The MAILBOX®

The Education Center®

grades K–1

W9-AES-321

Learning Centers

Our best learning center ideas from the 1995–2004 issues of *The Mailbox®* magazine

- **Literacy**
- **Science**
- **Dramatic Play**
- **Math**
- **Fine Motor**
- **Art**

Includes Colorful Ready-to-Go Pieces

Editorial Team: Becky S. Andrews, Kimberley Bruck, Karen P. Shelton, Diane Badden, Thad H. McLaurin, Sharon Murphy, Karen A. Brudnak, Juli Docimo Blair, Hope Rodgers, Dorothy C. McKinney

Production Team: Lori Z. Henry, Pam Crane, Rebecca Saunders, Jennifer Tipton Cappoen, Chris Curry, Sarah Foreman, Theresa Lewis Goode, Greg D. Rieves, Barry Slate, Donna K. Teal, Zane Williard, Tazmen Carlisle, Marsha Heim, Lynette Dickerson, Mark Rainey

www.themailbox.com

©2006 The Mailbox®
All rights reserved.
ISBN10 #1-56234-721-7 • ISBN13 #978-156234-721-5

Manufactured in the United States
10 9 8 7 6 5 4 3 2 1

Table of Contents

Concepts of Print 4

Phonological Awareness & Phonics ...8

Word Skills & Vocabulary 33

Reading 56

Language Conventions 58

Writing 62

Number & Operations 68

Measurement 95

Geometry 103

Graphing 106

Patterning................................109

Science 112

Fine Motor 122

Art 125

Dramatic Play 127

Sammie's Greenhouse

Skills Overview

Creative Arts

art media	125, 126
dramatic play	127, 128

Fine Motor

copying figures, Geoboard	123
hammering	124
squeezing	123, 124
tracing	126
using play dough	122

Literacy

Concepts of Print

letter formation	4
letter identification	4
letter matching: lowercase	5
letter matching: uppercase and lowercase	6

Phonological Awareness & Phonics

initial consonant sounds	10, 11
letter-sound association	9, 10, 11
onsets	15, 16
rhyming	8
rimes	15, 16
short-vowel words	13
vowels	12, 13, 14

Word Skills & Vocabulary

ABC order	43
antonyms	42
color words	33, 34, 122
compound words	42
name recognition	37
number words	34, 35, 36, 71
spelling	38, 39, 40, 41
word formation	40

Reading

reading motivation	56
word recognition	38, 39, 57

Language Conventions

capitalization	58, 59, 60
punctuation	59, 60
sentence structure	59, 60
word order	59

Writing

caption	65
description	66
friendly letter	65
list	62
prompt, picture	64
prompt, written	63, 64
response	62
specific purpose	63

Math

Number & Operations

addition facts	73, 77, 78
addition sentences	74
addition with manipulatives	75, 76
counting	69, 75
fact families: addition and subtraction	78
fractions: recognizing halves	79
modeling numbers	69, 70, 71, 72
number identification	69
number order	68, 69
numerals: sets	70
numerals: sets, number words	36, 71
odd and even numbers	80
place value	80
skip-counting	72
subtraction	74, 78

Measurement

capacity, estimating	96
length, comparing & ordering	95
length: nonstandard units	95
money: coin combinations	97
money: equivalent amounts	97

Geometry

shapes, identifying	103
shapes, recognizing	103

Graphing

bar graph	106
picture graph	106

Patterning

copy a pattern	109, 110, 124
create a pattern	110, 111
describe a pattern	111
extend a pattern	109
number patterns	111

Science

animals, categorizing	113
colors, mixing	123, 126
plants, categorizing	112
plants, observing	112
seasons	114
sink or float	113

Concepts of Print

Letter Hopscotch

Want your little ones to practice **letter identification?** Hop to it and try this center idea! Draw boxes on your sidewalk or blacktop area to make a hopscotch pattern. Label each box with a letter of the alphabet. Give a child a beanbag. Have her toss the beanbag onto a letter, identify the letter, and then read the other letters as she hops through the pattern. As a variation, label the boxes with sight words. Hop to it!

Maureen Behrs
Linkhorne Elementary
Lynchburg, VA

Letter Detectives

Youngsters will be keeping one another in suspense as they practice **letter formation** in your literacy center! Provide a variety of materials, such as craft sticks, toothpicks, wooden cubes, pipe cleaners, and clay. Also provide a stack of large index cards, each with a different letter written on it. Have each child at the center choose a material and a letter card, without letting others at the center see his chosen letter. Have each child use his material to form the letter on his card. Then, one by one, have youngsters show their handiwork to the others. Have your little letter detectives determine which letter each child formed.

Dayle Timmons
Chets Creek Elementary
Jacksonville Beach, FL

Letters and Feathers

Letter-matching skills take flight with this center idea! Duplicate the turkey pattern on page 7. Color and cut out the head; then glue it to the center of a paper plate. Add colored dot stickers around the top edge of the plate. Then program the plate and a set of wooden clothespins as shown. Direct youngsters to match the letters by clipping a clothespin on its corresponding dot. For a variation, program the plate with lowercase letters and the clothespins with uppercase letters. Then have students match uppercase and lowercase letters in the same manner.

Helaine Donnelly
Washington School
Plainfield, NJ

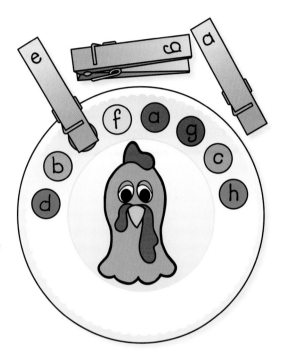

Alphabet Lollipops

Letter matching has never been sweeter than with this center. To begin, glue 26 library pockets onto a sheet of poster board. Label each pocket, in sequence, with a different letter of the alphabet. To make alphabet lollipops, label each of 26 construction paper circles with a different letter; then laminate them for durability. Attach each circle to a craft stick. To use the center, have a child place each lollipop into its corresponding pocket. Throughout the year, you might replace the round lollipops with seasonal shapes—such as apples, bears, hearts, or flowers.

Jacinda Unruh
Kids Kampus
McPherson, KS

Concepts of Print

Flip Your Lid

Reinforce **uppercase and lowercase letter recognition** with this easy-to-make, matching game. In advance, collect 26 milk jug lids. Use a permanent marker to label each lid with a different lowercase letter. To make a gameboard, use the pattern on page 7 to make 26 apple cutouts. Label each cutout with a different uppercase letter and glue them to a poster board grid as shown.

To play the game, a student matches each lid to its corresponding apple. For more fun, set a timer to see how quickly a child can match the letters. Can he improve his game time?

Jacinda Unruh
Kids Kampus
McPherson, KS

A	B b	C	D
E	F	G	H
I	J	K	L
M	N	O	P
Q	R	S	T
U	V	W	X
	Y	Z	

Miniblinds

Save those old miniblinds for this **uppercase and lowercase letter-matching** activity that also develops fine-motor skills. To prepare, remove the slats from a set of miniblinds. Use a permanent marker to program several slats with uppercase letters and several slats with lowercase letters. Then program spring-type clothespins with corresponding letters. Place the clothespins in a basket. Place the miniblind slats and the basket in a center. To use this center, a child chooses a clothespin, reads the letter, and clips it to the corresponding letter on a slat.

Ardy Nelson
Highland Public School
Highland, WI

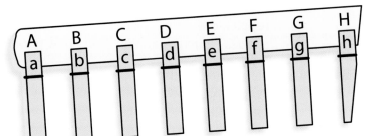

Apple Patterns
Use with "Flip Your Lid" on page 6 and "Apple-Pickin' Time" on page 13.

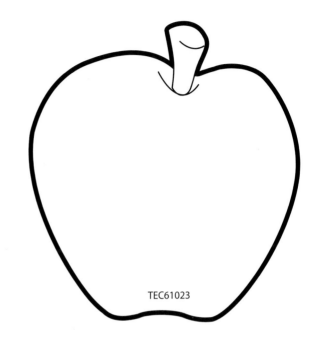

Turkey Pattern
Use with "Letters and Feathers" on page 5.

The Rhyming Box

The timing for **rhyming** is now! In advance, save a small box or container, such as a disposable wipe container. Collect party trinkets, old game pieces, and small toys. Look through the collection for rhyming pairs. For example, you might have a house and a mouse. Place the rhyming pairs in the box or container. Label the front of the container with "The Rhyming Box." Place the container in a center. To use this center, a child chooses an item from the container, and then tries to find an item that rhymes with the first one. It's rhyme time!

Cindy Fragosa-Johnston
Meadowbrook Elementary School
Fort Worth, TX

Rhyme Time

Create a taste for **rhymes** with cookie cutouts! Cut out five large cookie shapes from tan paper and 25 chocolate chip shapes from brown or cream-colored paper. Sort five chips onto each cookie. Program each cookie set with six rhyming words and then code the backs of the cutouts for self-checking. Laminate the pieces for durability and store them in a clean and empty cookie mix box. Place the box at a center. A student sorts the chips onto the cookies and then she flips the cutouts to check her work. If desired, keep a tin of edible cookies on your desk and reward each child who completes the center with the real thing!

Donna Zeffren
Torah Prep School
St. Louis, MO

Hanging Out From *A* to *Z*

Reinforce **initial sounds** at this kid-pleasing center. Use the T-shirt pattern on page 17 to create a tagboard template. Also write each letter of the alphabet on a slip of paper. Store the paper slips in a container; then place the container, the template, a supply of 9" x 12" pastel-colored construction paper, pencils, scissors, glue, markers, discarded magazines, and a laundry basket at a center. A student traces the T-shirt template on construction paper and cuts the shape out. Then he draws an alphabet letter from the container and writes that letter on his T-shirt cutout. Next, the student decorates his cutout with pictures of items that begin with the letter's sound. The pictures may be illustrated or cut from the magazines at the center. When the projects are dry, place them in the basket and invite students to order the T-shirts alphabetically.

Julie Earthal
Thomas Jefferson Elementary
Alton, IL

An Ever-Changing Caterpillar

Most caterpillars come and go, but this one just keeps changing—its **letter sound,** that is! Design a caterpillar head and display it on the wall above a center. Beside the caterpillar head, mount a laminated speech bubble and use a wipe-off marker to program the bubble with a letter sound. At the center you will also need scissors, crayons or markers, masking tape, and a supply of nine-inch construction-paper circles. A child labels the circle with a word and/or picture that has the featured sound. He then uses masking tape to attach his work to the caterpillar. When it's time to change the caterpillar, remove the circular body sections and reprogram the speech bubble with a different letter sound.

Marie Stoner
Bowers School
Massillon, OH

Look What's Buzzin'

Letter sounds will be the buzz at this phonics-related center. For each letter that you would like to include, photocopy the bee pattern and the honey-jar pattern (page 18) on construction paper. Color the bees with markers; then cut out the patterns. Program each bee with a letter. Then, for each letter, cut out a magazine picture with the same beginning sound. Glue each magazine picture to a honey jar and laminate the patterns if desired. Place the bees and the honey jars in a center. To use this center, a child matches each bee to the corresponding honey jar. (Program the backs of the honey jars for self-checking if desired.)

Melissa Iverson
Academy Park Elementary
Bountiful, UT

Consonant Kites

Beginning-sound practice takes flight in this center. Label a colorful construction paper kite for each letter *k, l, s,* and *t.* Cut out the bows on pages 19 and 21. Then glue each bow to a spring-type clothespin. Tape a length of curling ribbon to the bottom of each kite. Store the kites and bows in a center. To do this activity, a child matches the bows to the corresponding kite's tail. Let's go fly a consonant kite!

Trish Draper
Millarville Community School
Millarville, Alberta, Canada

Phonological Awareness & Phonics

Clip It!

Students will think this **initial-consonant** center is a snap! Cut out the picture cards from page 23. Then, laminate the cards and store them in a resealable plastic bag. Next program a spring-type clothespin for each consonant letter. Place the clothespins and the bag of cards at a center. A student removes the cards from the bag. One at a time he reads each card, clips a clothespin onto the card to complete the word, and flips the card to verify that the word he spelled matches the word written on the back. Then he removes the clothespin and completes the next card.

Melinda Casida
Crowley Elementary
Visalia, CA

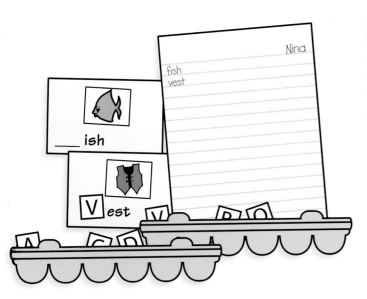

Missing Sounds

Put students hot on the trail of missing sounds at this **phonics center!** Cut out the picture cards on page 25. Glue each card to the top of a 3" x 5" card and program the bottom of the card to reinforce desired phonics skills. Then use a permanent marker to program the back of each card for self-checking. Store the cards at a center along with a set of sorted letter tiles, writing paper, and pencils. For each card, a student names the picture and places on the card the tile(s) needed to make the missing sound. Then she copies the resulting word on her paper and flips the card to check her work.

Maureen Pickle
Saltville Elementary School
Saltville, VA

A Vowel Search

Youngsters will be on the lookout for **vowels** in this activity. Stock the literacy center with newspapers, construction paper, highlighters, scissors, and glue. (Be sure to preview the newspapers to make sure there's no inappropriate content.) Instruct each child to cut out several words that are in large print and glue them onto a sheet of paper. Then have him highlight all the vowels he recognizes in the cutouts. Once center time is over, gather the completed papers and have the whole group tally how many of each vowel was found. Do some vowels appear more often than others?

Jacqueline M. Futerman
Pleasant Day Kindergarten
Verona, NJ

Munch a Bunch of Vowels

Not one youngster will try to wiggle away from this **vowel** center! Place drawing paper, several circle tracers, pencils, and crayons or markers at a center. Add one or more task cards programmed with a vowel-related activity. A student chooses and reads an activity card. Then, using the supplies at the center, he draws a caterpillar on his paper. After decorating the caterpillar's head, the student programs the remaining body sections as described on the task card. He completes his project by adding desired details to his critter and coloring a scene around it.

Michelle Blaylock
Oviedo, FL

Vowel Task Card
Draw a caterpillar.
It needs a head and five body sections.

Color a face for the caterpillar.

In each body section, draw a picture of a short-vowel word. Write the word too.
You may use each short vowel only once.

Finish your picture.

Apple-Pickin' Time

Picking apples is the perfect way to reinforce the **long and short sounds of a.** Duplicate 24 apple shapes (patterns on page 7) on red construction paper. Program 12 apples with short /a/ words and 12 apples with long /a/ words. Next cut tree foliage and a tree trunk from colored paper. Glue the foliage and tree trunk onto a sheet of poster board, and write desired student directions and the title "Apple-Pickin' Time." Laminate the center components for durability, and cut them out. For self-checking, use a permanent marker to program the backs of the long /a/ cutouts. Place the apples in a basket; then store the basket and the poster board at a center. A student randomly places all the apples (faceup) on the tree; then she picks only the apples that are programmed with long /a/ words. To check her work, she flips over the apples she picked.

Betsy Liebmann
Gotham Avenue School
Elmont, NY

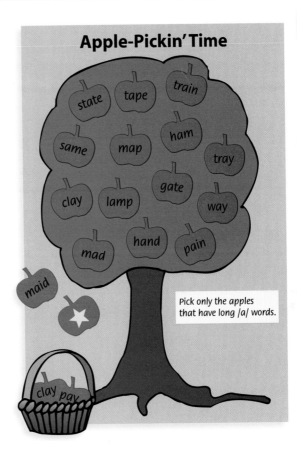

Apple-Pickin' Time

state · tape · train · same · map · ham · tray · clay · lamp · gate · way · mad · hand · pain · maid · clay · pay

Pick only the apples that have long /a/ words.

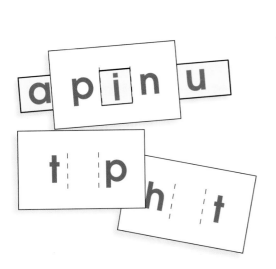

a · p · i · n · u

t · p · h · t

Very Important Vowels

Focus on **vowel sounds** with these changing word cards. Use a blue marker to program each of a supply of 3" x 5" index cards with a beginning and ending letter for a different three-letter word, as shown. Make a 1½-inch slit in the paper on both sides of the missing vowel. Then use a red marker to program a 1" x 9" strip of paper with the vowels.

To use the cards, a child slides the strip through the slits of one card so that a vowel completes the word. Then she reads the word on the card and determines if it is a real word or not. She then pulls the strip to change the vowel and make a new word. Encourage her to continue this process until she has read all possible words on each card.

Sherry Cook
Glenwood Springs, CO

Eggs in a Basket

Reinforce **short- and long-vowel sounds** at this "egg-stra" special center. From colorful tagboard, cut a supply of egg shapes. Label half of the cutouts with short-vowel words and the other half with long-vowel words. Code the backs of each set of eggs for self-checking. Place the eggs in a resealable plastic bag; then place the bag of eggs and a basket filled with cellophane grass at a center. A student removes the eggs from the plastic bag and places only the eggs bearing short-vowel words in the basket. To check his work, the student flips over each set of sorted eggs. What an "egg-ceptionally" fun way to practice vowel sounds!

adapted from an idea by Betsy Liebmann
Gotham Avenue School
Elmont, NY

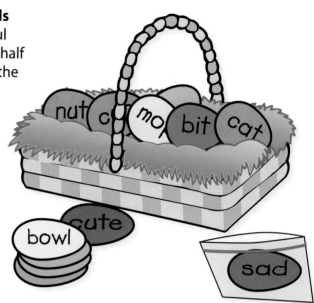

A Phonics Factory

Sounds, sounds, and more sounds are sorted at this kid-run factory! To create a **short-vowel** center, you will need six sorting bins. Label one bin "Rejects." Then cut out the labels from page 27 and tape one onto each remaining bin. Next, program a set of word cards to be sorted. Program five or more cards per bin. To make this center self-checking, code the backs of the cards that match with matching shapes. Store the cards in a decorated shoebox; then place the box and the sorting bins at a center. A student removes the cards from the box and sorts them into the appropriate bins. When she has finished sorting, she turns over the cards in each bin. If sorted correctly, the shapes on the backs of the cards will match.

Kristin McLaughlin
Boyertown Area Schools
Boyertown, PA

Phonological Awareness & Phonics

Fishy Words

Reel in practice with **onsets and rimes.** Cut four fishbowl shapes from construction paper. Cut a large oval from the center of each one and then discard the oval. Label each fishbowl with a rime. Also color and cut out a copy of the fish patterns on page 29. Laminate the fishbowls and fish, leaving intact the laminating film in the center of the fishbowls. Place the fishbowls and fish at a center stocked with paper and pencils.

A student reads the rime on a selected fishbowl. She finds a fish labeled with an onset that can be used with the rime to form a word. She places the fish on the fishbowl and then jots the word on her paper. After she identifies and writes the remaining word possibilities, she removes the fish, selects another fishbowl, and repeats the process.

adapted from an idea by Mary Beth Godbout
Gilford, NH

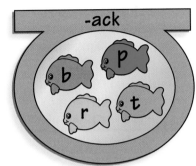

Rimes
-ack   -in
-est   -ot

Laticia
back
pack
rack
tack

Word Family Houses

Students will feel right at home with this **word family** (rime) activity. To review three rimes, gather three empty cube-shaped tissue boxes. Cover the sides of each box with colorful paper, then decorate the box to resemble a house. Label each house with a different rime. Cut out pictures that represent the rimes from discarded workbooks and magazines. Glue each cutout onto a small card. On the back of each card, write the corresponding word with the rime underlined. Laminate the cards and store them in a resealable plastic bag. Place the bag and the houses at a center. A student sorts the cards into the houses by naming each picture and identifying its rime. To check her work, she removes the cards from the house and verifies that the rime underlined on the back of each card is on the house.

Patty Scranton
Tallahassee, FL

15

Phonological Awareness & Phonics

"Chick" This Out

Beginning reading skills and **word family** practice are hatching in this center. Cut out a construction paper copy of the chick patterns on page 30. Also cut out the picture cards on page 31. Then invite your little peeps to hop on over and match each egg to its corresponding chick. Cheep, cheep!

Liz Mooney
Central Rayne Kindergarten
Rayne, LA

Letter by Letter

Students will be game for forming **word families** at this partner center! Program several blank cards with chosen rimes, formatting each card as shown. Place the cards, a container of letter tiles (consonants only), paper, and pencils at a center.

Each partner divides her paper into fourths. She takes a card and six letter tiles at random. She labels one section of her paper with her rime. She positions her letter tiles to form different words with the rime, listing each word in the labeled section of her paper. When both youngsters have exhausted their word-building possibilities, they trade cards to use different rimes in a similar manner. The youngsters compare their completed lists for each rime. Then they place their cards in a discard pile, return their letter tiles, and repeat the process to complete their papers.

adapted from an idea by Katy Hoh
WCK Walls School
Pitman, NJ

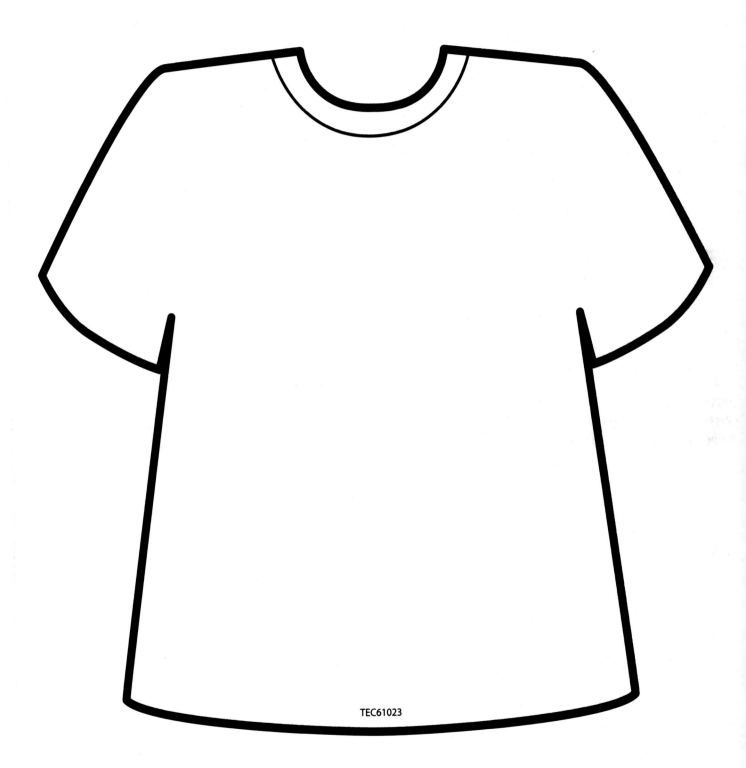

TEC61023

Bee and Honey Patterns
Use with "Look What's Buzzin'" on page 10.

TEC61023

TEC61023

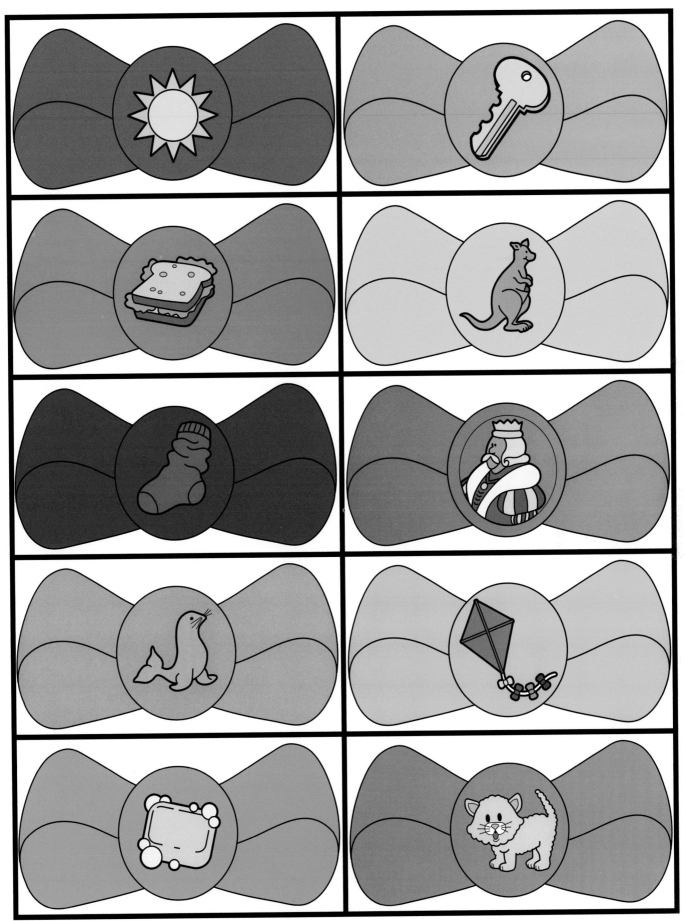

TEC61023

TEC61023

TEC61023

TEC61023

TEC61023

TEC61023

TEC61023

TEC61023

TEC61023

TEC61023

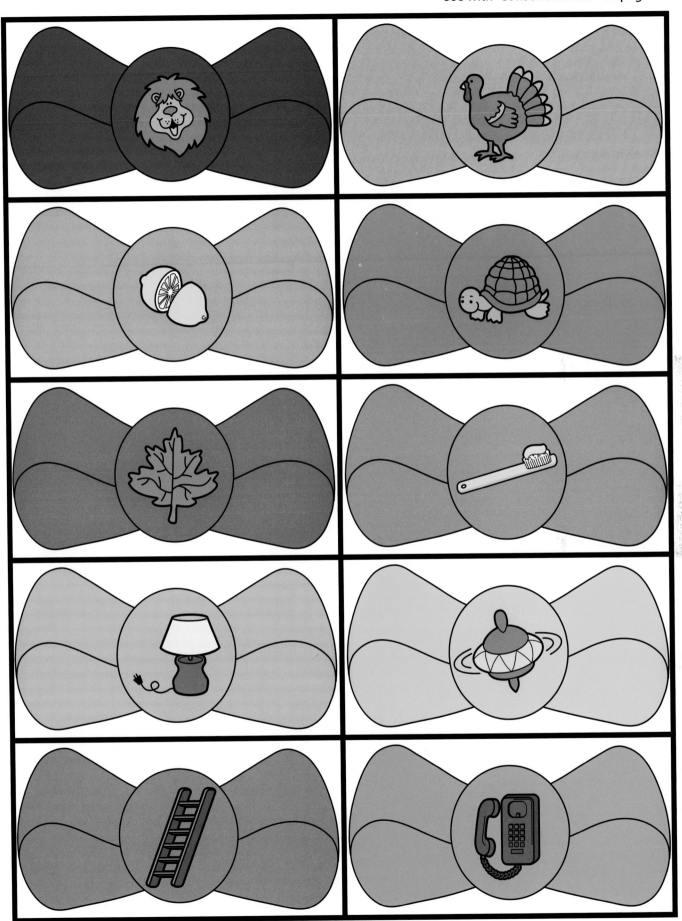

TEC61023

TEC61023

TEC61023

TEC61023

TEC61023

TEC61023

TEC61023

TEC61023

TEC61023

TEC61023

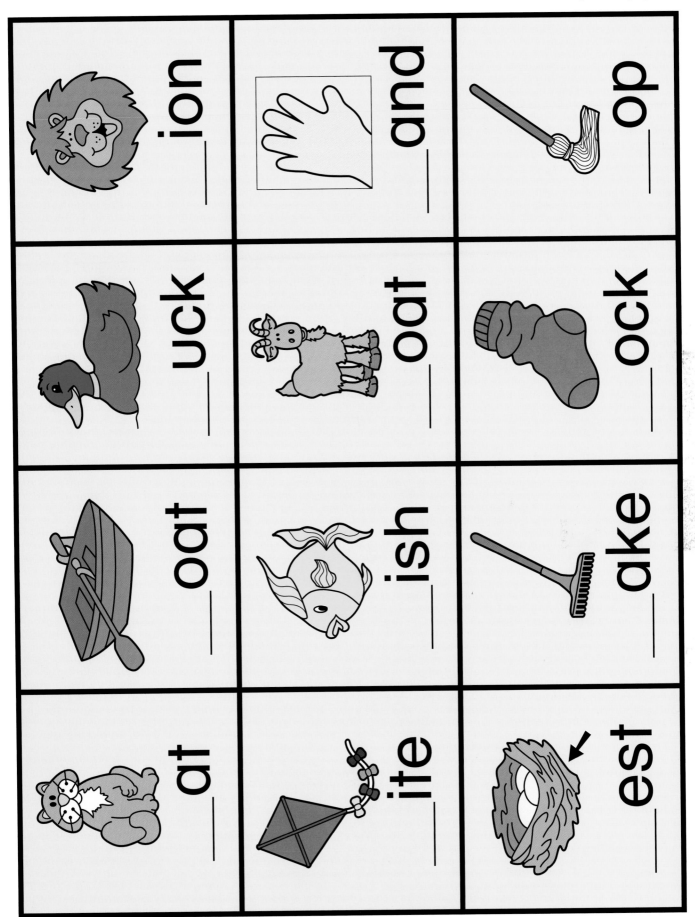

_ion

_and

_op

_uck

_oat

_ock

_oat

_ish

_ake

_at

_ite

_est

lion

duck

boat

cat

hand

goat

fish

kite

mop

sock

rake

nest

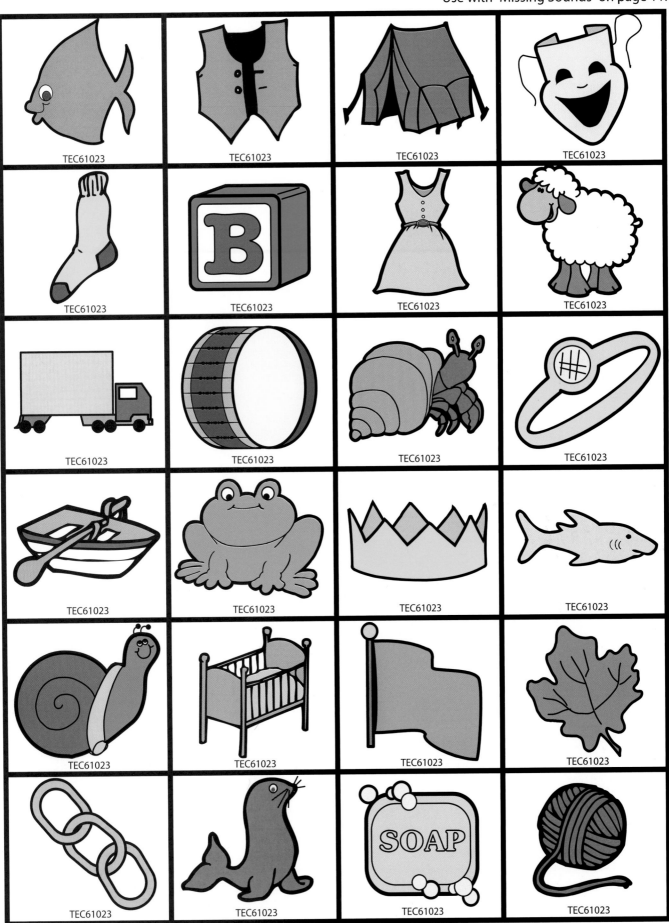

TEC61023   TEC61023   TEC61023   TEC61023

TEC61023   TEC61023   TEC61023   TEC61023

TEC61023   TEC61023   TEC61023   TEC61023

TEC61023   TEC61023   TEC61023   TEC61023

TEC61023   TEC61023   TEC61023   TEC61023

TEC61023   TEC61023   TEC61023   TEC61023

ŏ
sock

TEC61023

ă
apple

TEC61023

Phonics
Factory

TEC61023

ĭ
pig

TEC61023

ŭ
nut

TEC61023

ĕ
bed

TEC61023

b

TEC61023

n

TEC61023

t

TEC61023

bl

TEC61023

c

TEC61023

d

TEC61023

p

TEC61023

r

TEC61023

sp

TEC61023

sn

TEC61023

h

TEC61023

g

TEC61023

Chick Patterns

Use with "'Chick' This Out" on page 16.

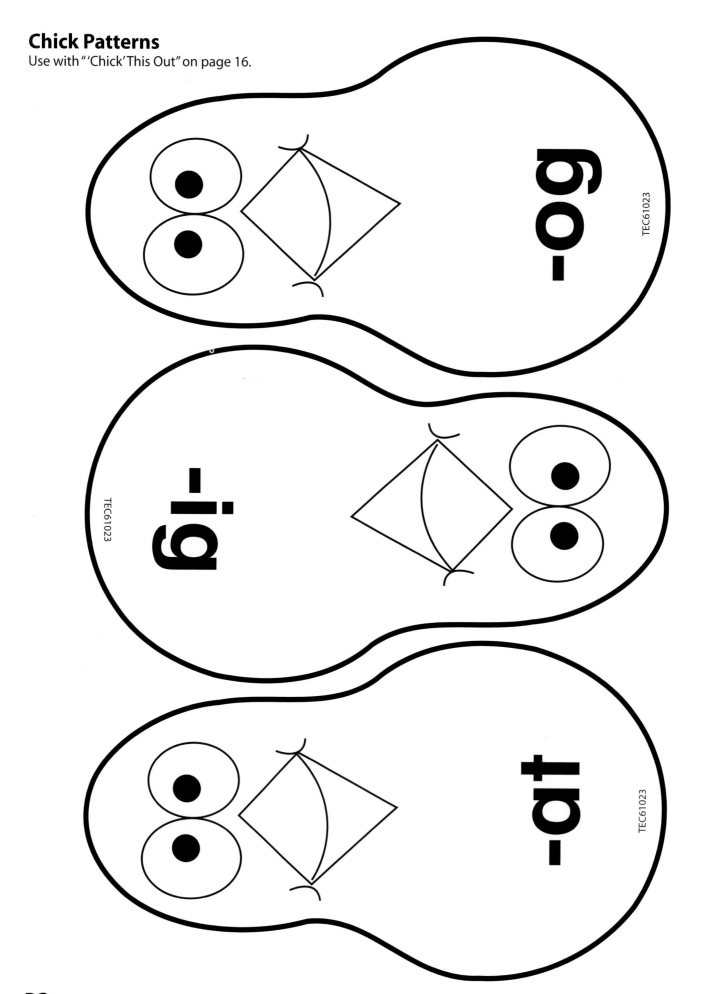

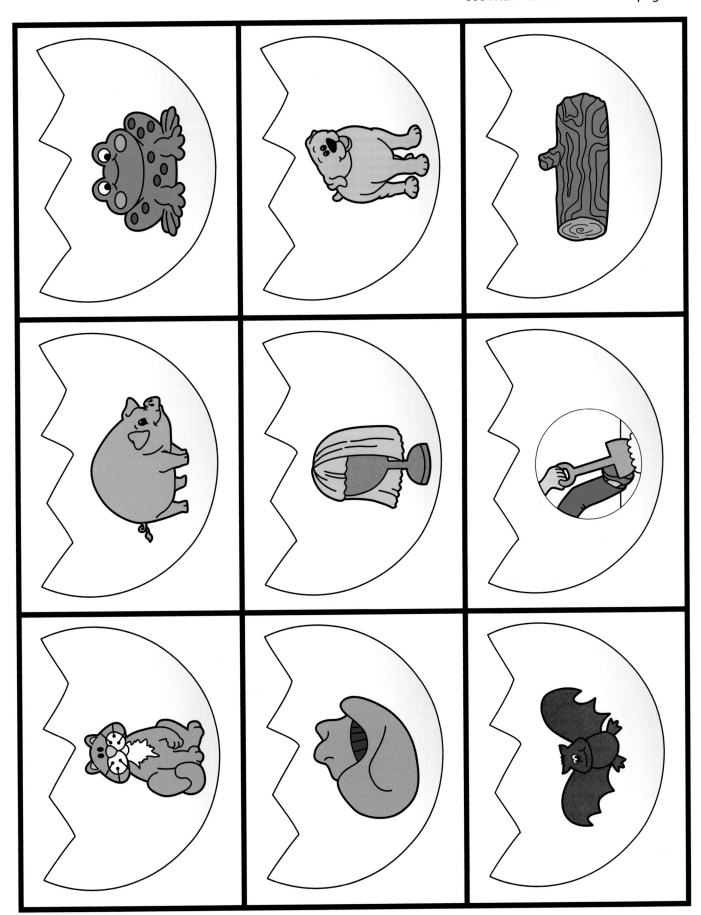

-og

TEC61023

-og

TEC61023

-og

TEC61023

-ig

TEC61023

-ig

TEC61023

-ig

TEC61023

-at

TEC61023

-at

TEC61023

-at

TEC61023

Whale of a Tail

Reinforce **color words** with this whale center. To make the center, duplicate the whale pattern (page 44) on construction paper. Program the head part of the pattern with a color word. Program the tail part of the pattern with a corresponding color splotch. Then puzzle-cut each of the whales. To use this center, a child matches each whale with the corresponding tail.

Cindy Stefanick
Roosevelt School
Worcester, MA

Take Flight!

Color-word recognition is on the rise with this visually oriented activity. For each color that you'd like to include, duplicate a hot-air balloon (from page 44) onto white construction paper. Color each basket—or glue on colored construction paper. Then color each balloon to match its basket. As you color, leave spaces (as shown) that correspond to the color-word's shape. Then write each corresponding color word on a separate piece of acetate. To do this activity, a child reads a color word on acetate, then places it on the appropriate balloon. If he is correct, the letters will fit inside the white space. If the letters do not fit in the space, he tries again.

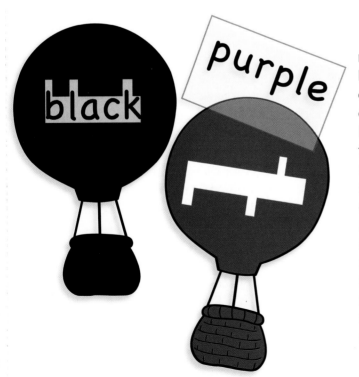

Word Skills & Vocabulary

Brushin' Up

Brush up **color-word recognition** with this artsy center activity. To prepare, photocopy a supply of the patterns on page 45. Color a different color of paint on each palette; then print a corresponding color word on each paintbrush. Color-code the back of each paintbrush for self-checking. Laminate and cut out the patterns. If desired, also use the patterns to decorate a string-tie envelope (as shown) and store all of the pieces in the envelope. To do this activity, have a child arrange all of the paint palettes on a flat surface. Then have him match each paintbrush to the corresponding palette. To check his work, a child simply turns over the paintbrush to look for matching colors.

adapted from an idea by Lara Renfroe
Heber Springs Elementary School
Heber Springs, AR

Jackets for Cats

"Purr-fect" **color-word and number-word recognition** is the goal of this dress-up activity. In advance, duplicate ten white construction paper copies of page 46. Cut out the patterns. Then color each jacket a different color. Program each cat with a different color word across its chest. Next, label one foot of each cat with a different number word from one to ten. Place the cats, jackets, and a container of large buttons at the center.

To complete the activity, a child dresses each cat with the appropriate colored jacket and then places the correct number of buttons on it. Ready, set—get dressed!

Lynne Nelson
Sherrills Ford Elementary School
Sherrills Ford, NC

Clippin' Clothes

Cut out several construction paper copies of the T-shirt pattern on page 17. Then label each one with a different **number word.** Put the clothing and a supply of colorful miniature plastic clothespins (found at craft and discount stores) at your math center. A child reads the number word and attaches the corresponding number of clothespins to the garment.

Brenda S. Beard
Greenbrier Elementary
Greenbrier, TN

Octopus Outfit

Number-word skills are hard at work with this eight-legged idea! Cut out construction paper copies of pages 47 and 48. Place the octopus body and legs in a center, along with 36 small suction cups (available at craft stores) or cereal pieces. To use this center, a child reads the number word on a leg, matches it to the correct numeral on the octopus body, then adds the correct number of suction cups. Your students will outfit this octopus in no time!

Trish Draper
Millarville Community School
Millarville, Alberta, Canada

Word Skills & Vocabulary

April Showers

Use these showers to reinforce **number-word recognition.** For each number that you'd like to include, photocopy an umbrella pattern (page 49) on construction paper. Program each umbrella with a different number word; then cut out a supply of construction paper raindrops. Laminate all the pieces; then store them in a decorated string-tie envelope. To do this activity, have a child arrange all of the umbrellas. Then ask him to place the corresponding number of raindrops over each umbrella.

adapted from an idea by Cris Edwards
Helena, AL

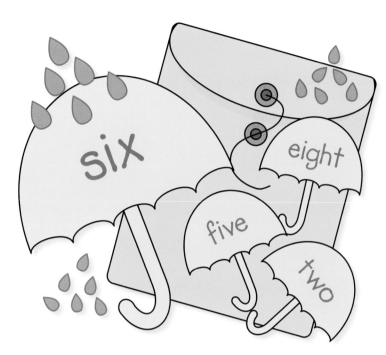

Flower Power

Number-word and number recognition is in this "kinder-garden." To make this center, photocopy the flower, stem, and pot patterns (page 50) for each number that you'd like to include. Program each flower with a number word, each stem with a dot set, and each pot with a numeral. Color the patterns; then cut them out. To do this activity, a child sequences the pots, then matches each corresponding stem and flower.

Shelley Banzhaf
Maywood Public School
Maywood, NE

Leafy Names

What's more fun than jumping in a pile of fresh fall leaves? Writing your **name** with leaves! For each child, pencil her name in the middle of a sheet of poster board. Place the poster boards in your art center along with a collection of colorful leaves and acorns. Invite each student to find her poster board, and then glue pieces of the fall foliage onto the letters and the background (similar to illustration shown). When all the projects are finished, mount them on a wall or bulletin board to create a "fall-bulous" display!

Shannon Garms
Garland, TX

Names in Newsprint

This center idea is just off the press to help students recognize the letters in their **names.** On a piece of tagboard, use a colored marker to write a child's name in big block letters. Place the name cards in a center along with old newspapers and magazines. Then direct each student to search through the provided materials to find the letters in her name. Have her cut out the letters and glue them on her name card as shown. To add tactile clues, glue yarn around each letter. Show off these newsworthy names by mounting each child's name card and photograph on a bulletin board.

Tracey Quezada
Varnum School
Lowell, MA

Word Skills & Vocabulary

Dig It!

Spelling at the sand table? Sure! Bury a large supply of magnetic letters in the sand of your sand table. Near the table, place a magnetic board with sight words or vocabulary words you want students to learn. Have a child choose a card and then dig for the letters needed to spell it on the magnetic board.

Jean Ricotta
Signal Hill Elementary
Dix Hills, NY

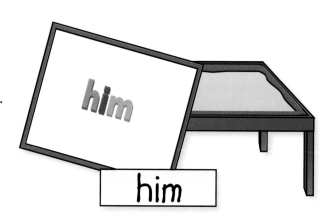

Popcorn Words

Here's a twist on discovery bottles that will have your students popping with excitement about **familiar words!** Fill a completely dry soda bottle about three-fourths full with popcorn kernels. Sketch a large bowl on a sheet of paper. Next, use the patterns on page 51 as templates to cut popcorn shapes from white craft foam. Label each one with a sight word; then slip them into the bottle. Tightly secure the bottle top and give the bottle a shake! Write all the words you've hidden in the bottle on the bowl. Duplicate the list; then put the copies in your reading center along with the bottle of popcorn words. Each time a child finds a word inside the bottle, she reads it. Then she highlights the word on her copy of the list.

Jo Montgomery
John C. French Elementary
Cuero, TX

Word Skills & Vocabulary

The Garden of Reading

Word skills will blossom with this center! Color six copies of the sun-and-flowers mat on page 52. Also cut out six of the picture cards on page 53. Write individual letters on the flowers to spell each picture word, as shown.

To use this center, a child sounds out the word on a mat and then chooses the corresponding picture and places it on the sun. After he has matched all the words and pictures, he has his teacher check his work.

Linda Havens and Lyn Edwards
Oakwood Elementary
Kalamazoo, MI

Shake and Spell

Shake up **spelling** with this center idea! Cover the outside of a large canister with construction paper or Con-Tact covering. Cut out six picture cards from page 53 and tape them on the outside of the can. Put the magnetic letters needed to spell each picture word inside the can; then put on the lid. Have a child shake the can and spill the letters out onto a tabletop. Then have him arrange the letters to spell each word depicted on the can.

Jeanne Jackson
Northside Primary
Palestine, TX

Word Skills & Vocabulary

Weekly Mystery Word

Your supersleuths will have a ball **forming words** at this center! Each week select a mystery word that relates to a current topic of study. In each of several resealable plastic bags, place construction paper squares labeled with the letters needed to spell the mystery word. Place the bags of letters, pencils, stickers, and writing paper at the center. Also post a laminated sign, like the one shown, that can be reprogrammed each week with an appropriate word goal. A student removes the letters from a plastic bag and manipulates them to make words. He writes each word he makes on his paper. He also tries to discover the mystery word by arranging all the letters in his bag to make one word. If he meets the posted goal, he attaches a sticker to his paper!

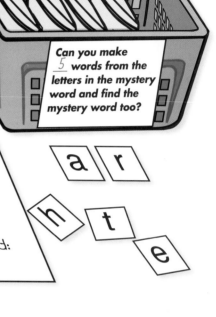

Lisa Kelly
Wood Creek Elementary School
Farmington, MI

Shape and Spell

Put your youngsters in touch with their **spelling** words with this handy activity. Using a wipe-off marker, program a decorated poster with your weekly spelling words. Place the programmed poster and a supply of colorful play dough at a center. A child uses the play dough to shape the letters needed to spell each word. Each week reprogram the center poster with current spelling words. How handy!

Tonya Byrd
E. Melvin Honeycutt Elementary
Fayetteville, NC

Word Skills & Vocabulary

Clip and Spell

Stir up an interest in weekly **spelling** practice at this partner center! Program a spring-type clothespin for each letter of the alphabet. Label extra clothespins for frequently used letters. Store the clothespins and a paint stick in a bucket; then place the container and a copy of the weekly spelling list at a center. One student becomes the *caller,* and his partner is the *speller.* The caller says the first word on the list and then watches closely as his partner spells the word by clipping clothespins onto the paint stick. If the correct spelling is given, the speller removes the clothespins from the paint stick, and the caller reads aloud the next word on the list. If an incorrect spelling is given, the caller repeats the word, and the partners work together to spell it. After each word on the list is correctly spelled, the partners change roles and repeat the activity.

Amy Ekmark
Eastside Elementary
Lancaster, CA

Spelling List
bump
duck
truck
up
cup
bus

Spelling Conversations

Spelling practice is loads of fun at this telephone center! You will need two disconnected or play telephones, a list of phone numbers that includes an assigned number for each student in the class, two notepads, pencils, and a copy of the weekly spelling list. Students visit the center in pairs. To begin, one youngster dials his partner's number and makes a ringing sound. When his partner answers, the student asks him to spell a word from the weekly spelling list. The partner writes the word on his message pad; then he spells it aloud. The original caller checks the spelling against the provided list. If the word is spelled incorrectly, he notifies his partner of his mistake and asks him to respell the word. Then the students reverse roles and repeat the activity. Play continues in this manner until each student spells a predetermined number of words.

Kristin McLaughlin
Boyertown Area Schools
Boyertown, PA

Compound Critters

Youngsters are sure to go buggy over **compound words** at this center! Cut five black circles (ladybug heads) and 20 identical red semicircles (ladybug wings) from construction paper. For each compound word listed, program a left and right wing with the corresponding word parts (see the illustration). Laminate the cutouts for durability. Place them at a center along with paper and pencils. To form five compound words, a student arranges the selected cutouts to resemble ladybugs. He writes the words on his paper. Then he uses the remaining cutouts to form five different words and adds them to his list.

Noelle B. Fell
Coyote Canyon Elementary School
Bullhead City, AZ

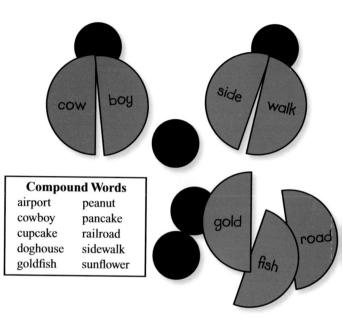

Compound Words	
airport	peanut
cowboy	pancake
cupcake	railroad
doghouse	sidewalk
goldfish	sunflower

Mitten Matchup

Warm up your youngsters' **antonym skills** with a handful of mittens! Use the mitten patterns from page 51 to make an even number of colorful construction-paper mittens. Program every two mittens with a pair of antonyms. Laminate the mitten patterns for durability and then cut them out. For self-checking, use a permanent marker to draw the same symbol on the back of each mitten in a matched pair. Store the cutouts and a supply of clothespins at a center. A student finds a match for each mitten and clips the pair together with a clothespin. To check her work, she flips the mitten pairs.

Amy Ekmark
Eastside Elementary
Lancaster, CA

Word Skills & Vocabulary

ABC Egg Basket

Hatch plenty of **alphabetizing** practice at this seasonal center. Tuck cellophane grass and six different-colored plastic eggs in a basket. For each egg, label four color-coded construction paper cards (such as purple cards for a purple egg) with different words to alphabetize. Store each card set in its corresponding egg. Place the basket of eggs, paper, and pencils at a center. A student selects an egg and writes its color on her paper. Next she cracks open the egg, arranges the cards in ABC order, and copies the alphabetized words. Then she returns the cards to the egg and the egg to the basket. Provide an answer key for self-checking, if desired.

adapted from an idea by Dawn Schroeder
Kluckhohn Elementary
LeMars, IA

An Orderly Lineup

Students who hang out at this center reinforce **alphabetical order** skills. Suspend a clothesline (heavy string or lightweight cord) in a convenient and safe classroom location. Enlarge the patterns on page 55. Then make several construction paper copies, cut them out, and laminate them for reprogramming. Use a wipe-off marker to label the cutouts with words. Program the backs of the cutouts for self-checking. Store the cutouts in a laundry basket. Place this basket and a container of clothespins near the clothesline. A student clips the clothing items to the clothesline in sequential order and then checks the back of each cutout to verify her work. To reprogram the center, wash away the programming!

Ida Koll
Shadycrest Elementary
Pearland, TX

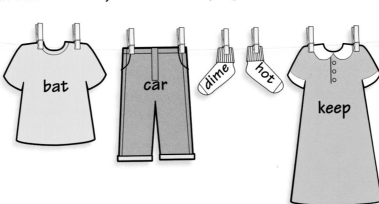

Whale Pattern
Use with "Whale of a Tail" on page 33.

TEC61023

Hot Air Balloon Pattern
Use with "Take Flight!" on page 33.

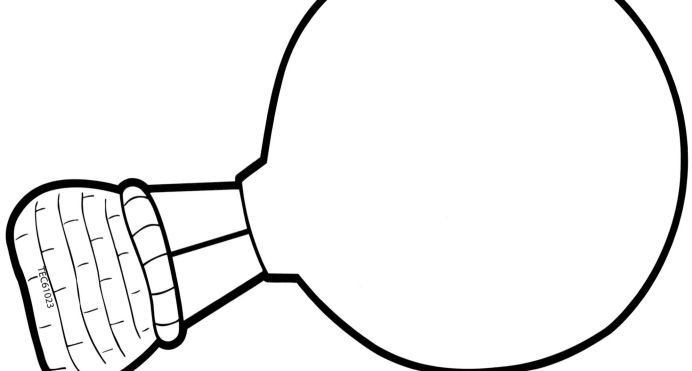

TEC61023

44

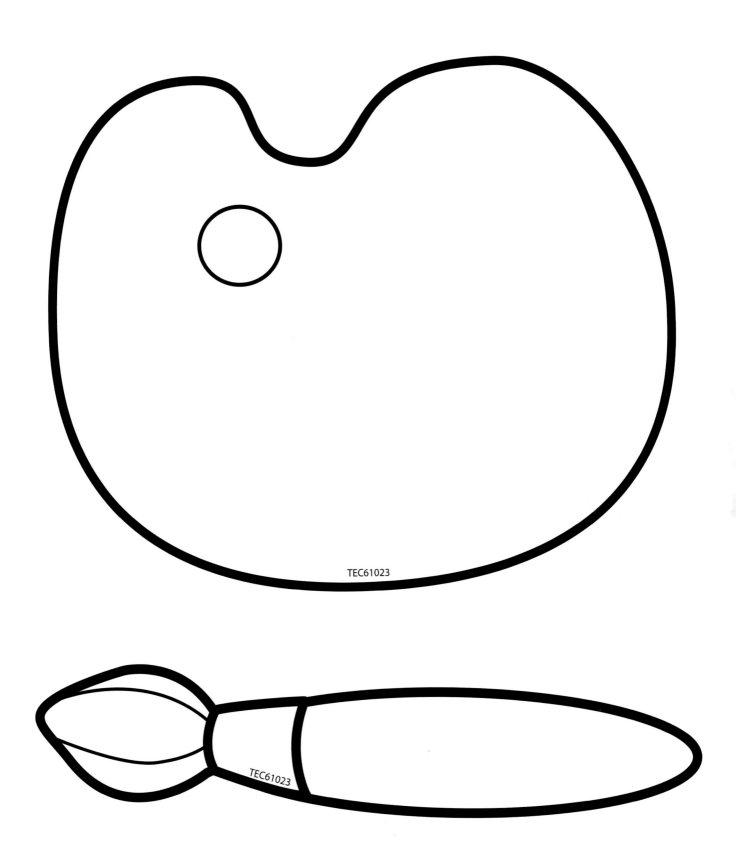

TEC61023

TEC61023

Cat and Jacket Patterns
Use with "Jackets for Cats" on page 34.

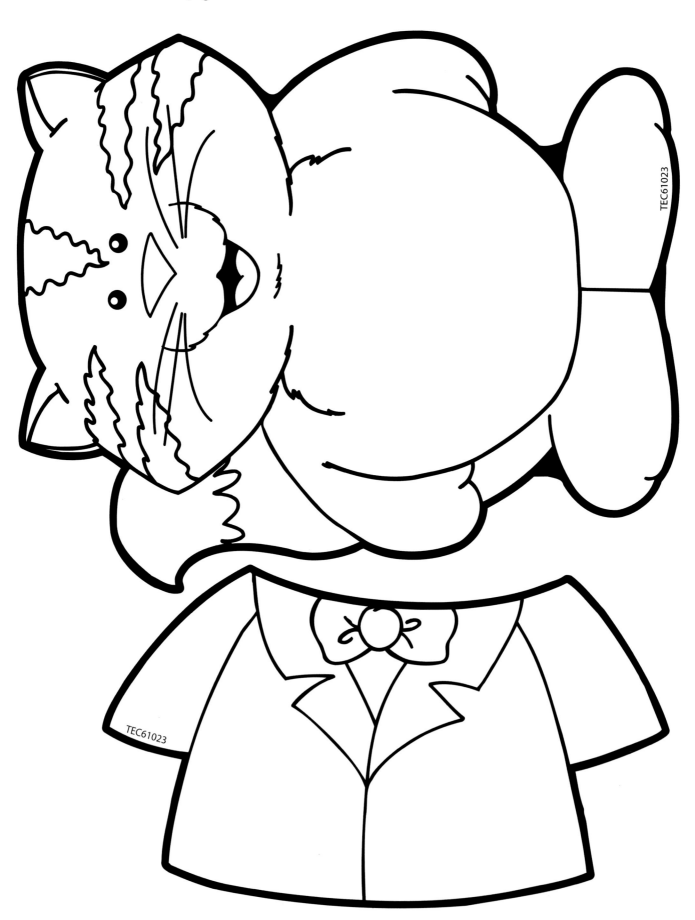

TEC61023

1 2 3 4 5 6 7 8

 one

TEC61023

Octopus Leg Patterns
Use with "Octopus Outfit" on page 35.

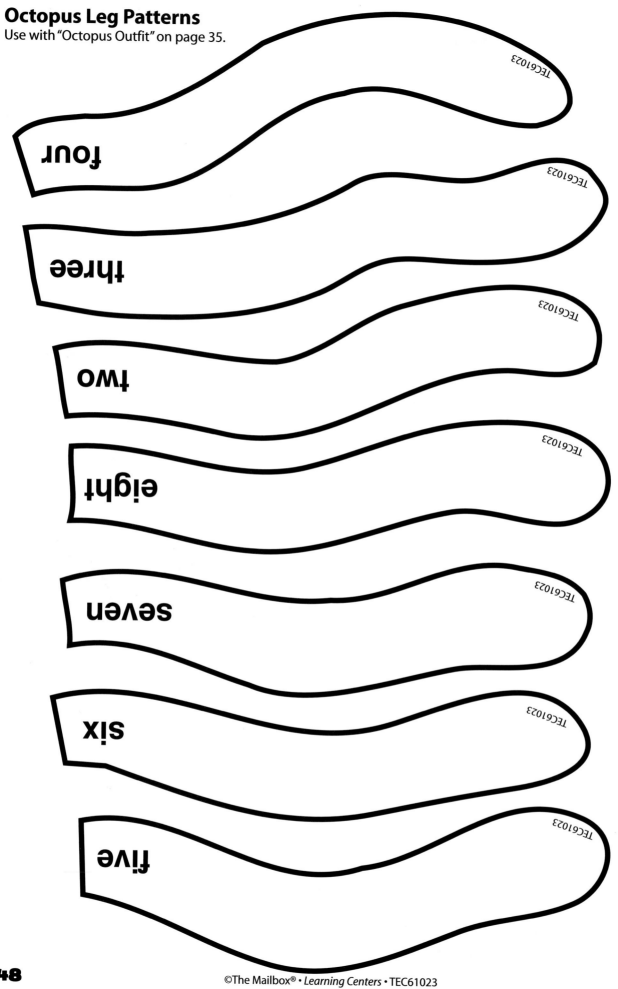

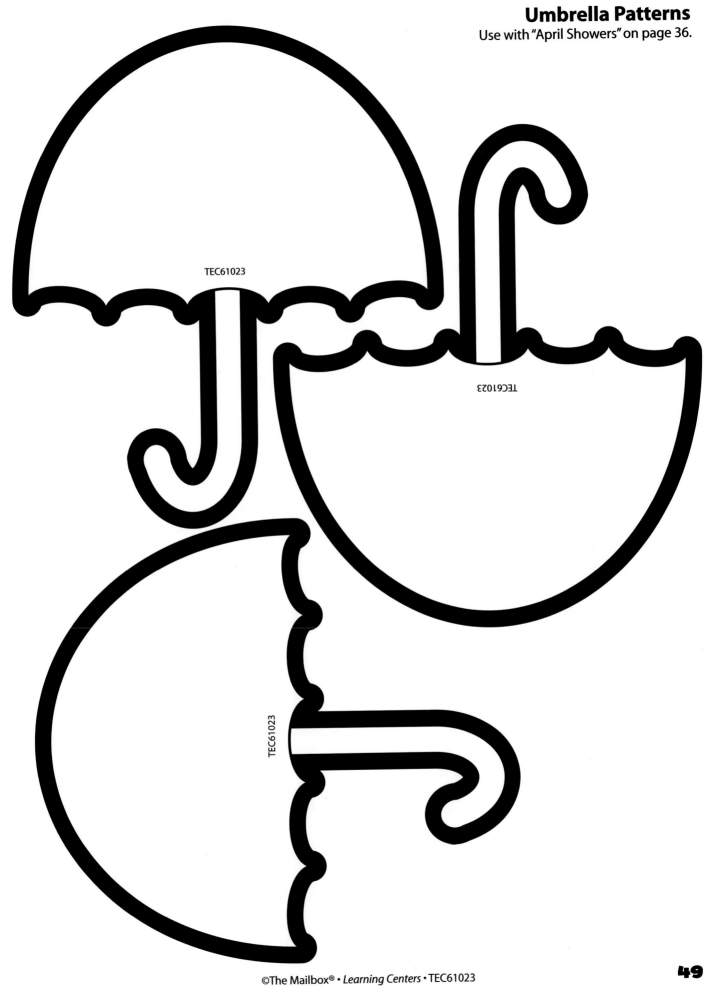

TEC61023

TEC61023

TEC61023

Flowerpot Patterns

Use with "Flower Power" on page 36.

Popcorn Patterns

Use with "Popcorn Words" on page 38.

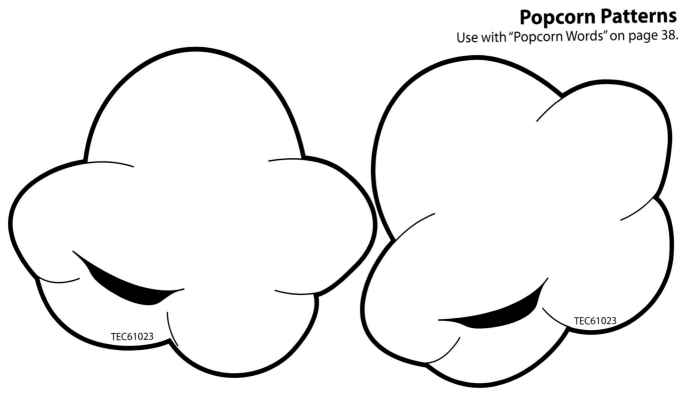

TEC61023

TEC61023

Mitten Pattern

Use with "Mitten Matchup" on page 42.

TEC61023

TEC61023

Note to the teacher: Use with "The Garden of Reading" on page 39.

Use any six cards with "The Garden of Reading" and the remaining six cards with "Shake and Spell" on page 39.

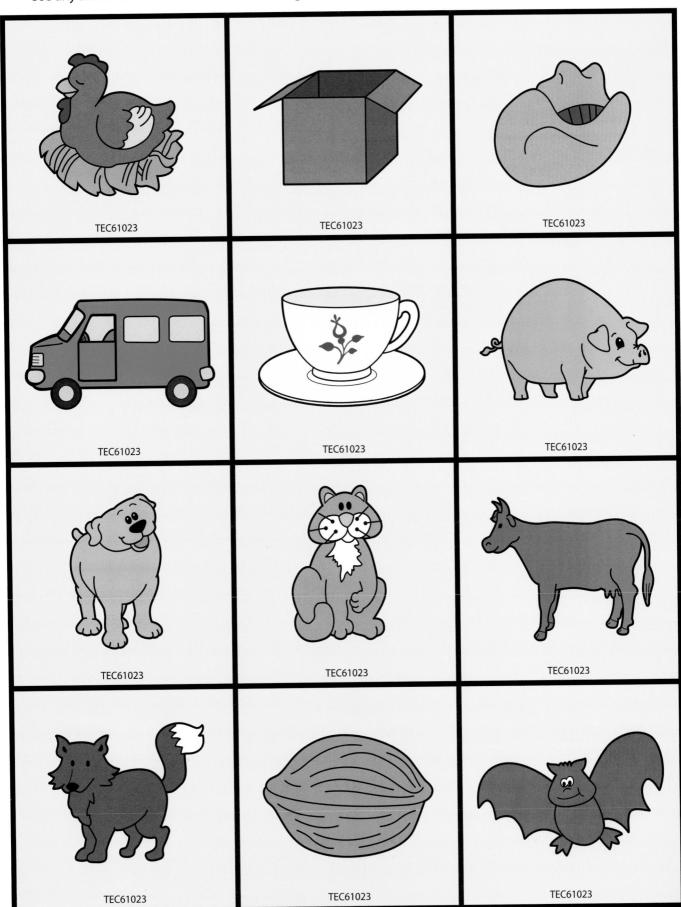

TEC61023

TEC61023

TEC61023

TEC61023

TEC61023

TEC61023

TEC61023

TEC61023

TEC61023

TEC61023

TEC61023

TEC61023

Reading

Reading Center With a Flair

Your **reading** center will invite youngsters into a world of imagination and adventure when you add seasonal and holiday accents to the area. For example, youngsters will immediately warm up to books in a beach reading center stocked with beach chairs, beach towels, beach bags, and sunglasses. During the fall, transform the center into a pumpkin patch complete with pumpkins, a bale of hay, and a scarecrow. During the winter holidays, decorate a Christmas tree and surround it with books. In January, try building a milk-carton igloo; then hang student-made snowflakes overhead. In the spring, provide picnic props and a picnic basket—full of books, of course! Change the center accents as often as you like to match any theme or occasion. Your creative seasonal flair will keep youngsters interested in the reading center all year long.

Catherine Matthews
First Baptist Learning Center
Tulsa, OK

The Reading Pool

With this suggestion you can transform your **reading** center into an oasis of learning. Position a small wading pool in your reading center; then toss in a few small decorative pillows. Cut out a palm tree from bulletin board paper and mount it on a wall near the center. Then cut out a few coconut shapes from construction paper and mount them on the tree. If desired, place a few artificial plants around the pool. Provide lots of sea-related literature for little ones to cozy up with in the reading pool. They'll be anxious to dive into a good book!

Jennifer Mitchell
New Caney Elementary
New Caney, TX

High-Flying Readers

Give your **beginning readers** a confidence boost at this nifty newspaper center. Place a supply of crayons and single newspaper pages at a center. A student chooses a newspaper page and uses a crayon to circle each word on the page that he can read. When the student has finished the page, he draws a black string from each circled word to create a balloon. Wow! Prepare for liftoff! These pages will definitely be a joy for your young readers and their parents to see!

Theodora Gallagher
Carteret School
Bloomfield, NJ

Time to Reminisce!

If you've gone on a field trip recently and taken photos—or will in the future—set up this center that helps children remember the good times they had and also reinforces **sequencing** events. Choose pictures from your collection that clearly show the sequence of events on your trip. Mount each picture on a construction paper background and describe the pictured event. Store the labeled photos in a resealable plastic bag; then place them in a center with a mat that is programmed with the name of the field trip. When a child visits this center, she reads the text and arranges the photos in sequential order.

Ann Scalley
Wellfleet, MA

Language Conventions

Undersea Decisions

Make a splash at this **capitalization** center! Mount an octopus cutout and eight sequentially numbered library pockets on blue poster board. Laminate the project for durability and then carefully reopen each pocket with an X-acto knife. Use a wipe-off marker to label one pocket with a lowercase letter and one with the upper-case version of the same letter. Label the six remaining pockets similarly, three featuring different letters. Select six words for each featured letter: three that require capital letters and three that do not. Next, write the words on individual cards using only lower-case letters. On the back of each card write its corresponding pocket number. A child sorts the cards into the pockets. Then he removes the cards from each pocket and flips them over to check his work. To reuse the center, reprogram the pockets with different alphabet letters and/or make a new set of game cards.

Susan Brown
Palmyra Elementary School
Palmyra, VA

Sorting for Capitals

Warm up your youngsters' **capitalization** skills! Using all lowercase letters, program a supply of base-ball cutouts (page 61) with words that need capital letters and words that do not. Code the back of each baseball that needs a capital. Store the cutouts in a resealable plastic bag. Place the bag and an upside-down baseball cap at a center. A student sorts baseballs that need capital letters into the cap and those that do not into a discard pile. Then she flips both sets of cutouts to check her work.

Susan Brown
Palmyra Elementary School
Palmyra, VA

Language Conventions

Silly Sentences

This center is sure to be a treat for your emergent readers! To prepare, write **simple sentences** on different colors of sentence strips. Then cut the words apart to form puzzles. (Using the same puzzle cut between each part of speech will allow students to mix up the words to build new sentences. See the illustration for clarity.) Also provide punctuation cards. Be sure to throw in some silly sentence options to keep reading fun!

Karen Smith
Pensacola, FL

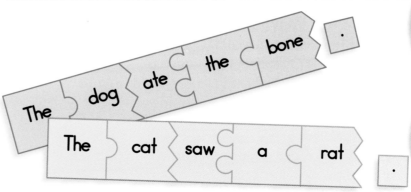

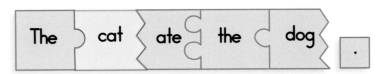

State-of-the-Art Sentences

Students can show their stuff again and again at this **sentence-writing** center! Use a colorful marker to label several craft sticks with nouns. Place the color-coded sticks in a container labeled "Nouns." Repeat the procedure to create color-coded sets of verbs and adjectives. Store the containers of craft sticks along with story paper, pencils, and crayons at a center. A student chooses a stick from each container and then uses the words on the sticks to create a state-of-the-art sentence. After he has written the sentence on his paper, he returns the craft sticks to the appropriate containers and illustrates his sentence.

Michelle Wolfe
Kennewick, WA

Language Conventions

Word by Word

Sentence writing is in the cards! Prepare two-sided word cards that include high-frequency words. To do this, label each side of a card with the same word—one side with the first letter capitalized and one side with the word in all lowercase letters. Also prepare a set of ending punctuation cards. File the word cards in a box divided by alphabetized tabs. File the punctuation cards behind a blank tab. Place the box, paper, and pencils at a center. A student arranges selected words on a work surface to make a complete sentence. He flips the cards as needed to ensure correct capitalization and adds the appropriate punctuation card. He writes the sentence on his paper and then refiles the cards. He repeats this process to write a specified number of sentences.

Sheila Criqui-Kelley
Lebo Elementary
Lebo, KS

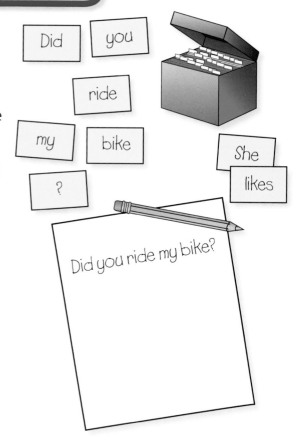

Pancakes, Anyone?

Adjectives add flavor at this **sentence-writing** center! Cut 12 circles from light brown construction paper to represent pancakes. Program each one with a different noun. Place the pancakes in a clean and empty pancake mix box. To represent butter pats, program each of 12 yellow construction paper squares with a different adjective. Place the butter pats in a small plastic dish. Set the dish and box at a center stocked with paper and pencils. A student takes at random two pancakes and two butter pats. She places a butter pat on each pancake. Then she writes a sentence for each adjective-noun pair, remembering to check her work for needed capitalization and punctuation.

Donna Zeffren
Torah Prep School
St. Louis, MO

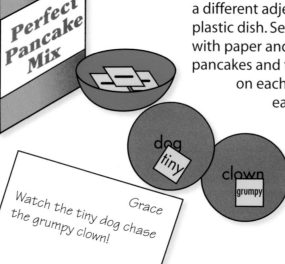

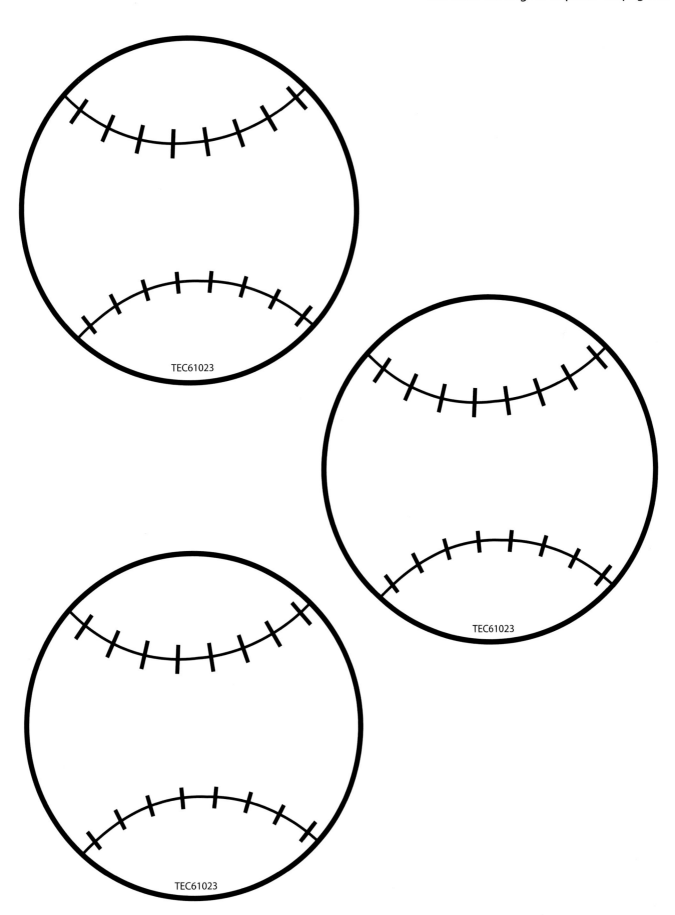

TEC61023

TEC61023

TEC61023

Picnic Grocery List

Who doesn't love going on a picnic in warm weather? Encourage young writers to prepare **lists** of what they'd like to take on a picnic! Stock your writing center with local grocery store flyers, pencils, and paper cut into long rectangles. Invite each child at this center to peruse the flyers, choose picnic items, and copy them down to make a list. Mmm! Let's eat!

Judi Lesnansky
New Hope Academy
Youngstown, OH

Kid Quotes

Give your **writing** center a new look with this picture-perfect idea. In advance, photograph each child. Glue the pictures to a sheet of poster board; then laminate it. Display the photo poster in the center along with a supply of speech-bubble cutouts. Write a simple question on a sentence strip and mount it above the poster. Have each student write her response to the question on a speech bubble and then tape it next to her picture. Change the question periodically to give your youngsters more writing practice.

Brenda Burns
Texarkana, TX

Let's Play Reporter!

Present some **purposeful writing** when you add reporter's forms to your writing center. Create forms for surveying or choosing favorites. Attach each form to a clipboard and invite students to choose an interesting topic. Then have each child get to work interviewing classmates and reporting on the classroom scene!

Julie Pressley
Fletcher Elementary
Fletcher, NC

Where Do All Those Teeth Go?

Brush up on students' **creative-writing** skills with this activity! Ask students to decide what they think the tooth fairy does with the teeth that she collects. Collectively decide on a few possible scenarios and write each one on a different tooth pattern. Tape each tooth pattern to a separate three-ring binder notebook. Place the notebooks, a hole puncher, pencils, and a supply of paper at a center. A student chooses a scenario and writes a more detailed version on a sheet of paper. When she is finished writing, she signs her name, hole-punches her paper, and places it in the corresponding notebook. When each student has completed the center, place the notebooks in the classroom library for everyone to read. No doubt you'll see lots of grins!

Writing

Calendar Creations

At this **writing** center, outdated calendars become picture-perfect writing prompts! To prepare a calendar, cover each monthly grid with colorful construction paper. Then cut a supply of writing paper to fit atop the construction paper pages. Place the writing paper, pencils, glue, and two or more prepared calendars at a center. A child selects a calendar picture that is opposite blank construction paper. He writes about the picture on writing paper and then glues his writing atop the construction paper. When all the construction paper pages of a calendar are filled, place the resulting booklet in the classroom library for all to enjoy!

Colette Walkins
Kingston Elementary School
Kingston, MA

Here's The Bait!

If you're fishing for **writing** ideas for your budding authors, you'll be hooked on this center! Using the patterns on page 67, duplicate a colorful supply of fish shapes. Label each fish with a different story starter; then laminate and cut out the patterns. Store the laminated fish cutouts in a plastic fishbowl. Place the bowl, story paper, pencils, and crayons at a center. A student chooses a fish from the bowl, copies the story starter on her paper, and returns the fish to the bowl. Then the student writes her story and illustrates her work. What a catch!

Vickie Crawford
Elkmont School
Elkmont, AL

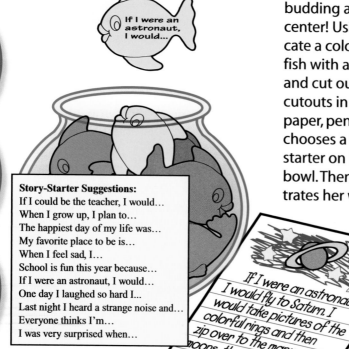

Story-Starter Suggestions:
If I could be the teacher, I would...
When I grow up, I plan to...
The happiest day of my life was...
My favorite place to be is...
When I feel sad, I...
School is fun this year because...
If I were an astronaut, I would...
One day I laughed so hard I...
Last night I heard a strange noise and...
Everyone thinks I'm...
I was very surprised when...

Homey Writing Center

Here's a cozy spot to help children feel right at home with **writing captions.** To make this center, staple construction paper strips to a board to resemble a window. Then add fabric curtains. Next staple or hot-glue a pad of drawing paper to the window. In the center, provide a supply of crayons, markers, and pencils. When a child visits this center, invite her to illustrate and write about what she'd like to see out the window. When she is finished, have her carefully tear her page off the top of the stack, leaving the next page ready for the next writer.

Kay Dawson
Newport News, VA

Keri

I see a big slide that goes to a pool.

You Have Mail!

Letter writing will be on the rise in your classroom when you include this motivating center. First decorate a box to serve as your class mailbox. Stock your writing center with a variety of writing and stationery supplies along with envelopes. Also provide a small name card for each child. In the center, post a list of various words and phrases that children are likely to use. When a child visits this center, encourage her to write a letter to a classmate. Have her write the recipient's name on an envelope, fold and insert her letter, and place it in the class mailbox. Next have her use reusable adhesive to attach the recipient's name card to the mailbox. As each student comes to this center, have her check the mailbox to see if she has mail. If she does, she removes her name card before reading her mail and then creates her own mail to send.

Deborah R. Kesel
Dundee Elementary
Dundee, FL

65

Writing

Picture-Perfect Memories

Use the photos you've taken during the school year at this **writing** center! Place the snapshots, pencils, crayons or markers, clear tape, a stapler, and half sheets of writing and construction paper at a center. A student selects a photo, describes her memory of the pictured event on writing paper, and staples her writing between two pieces of construction paper. Then she tapes the photo to the front cover and adds a title, her name, and other desired decorations. Now that's a picture-perfect memory!

Alyce Pearl Smith
Butzbach Elementary
Butzbach, Germany

Snapshot Memories

If you've been snapping photos of your students and other school-related events throughout the year, you can prepare this **writing** center in a snap too! On the first page of an inexpensive photo album, insert a title page that includes your name, the school's name, the dates of the school year, and the names of your students. Then, on each left album page, insert one snapshot that you've taken during the school year. Leave the last page in the album blank. Prepare as many of these photo albums as you like; then place the albums at a center along with a supply of writing paper that has been trimmed to fit the album pages. A student flips through the albums and chooses one photograph that he would like to write about. Then he inserts his completed writing into the album page opposite the photo. After each student has had an opportunity to write about a different photo, invite students to revisit the center until each featured photograph has been written about. On the last day of school, look through the albums with your students and ask each student to read aloud his written contribution(s).

Karen Walden
Ravenel Elementary
Seneca, SC

Fish Patterns

Use with "Here's the Bait!" on page 64 and "By the Number" on page 68.

Number & Operations

Dot-to-Dot and Count a Lot!

Help your kindergartners practice counting and **number sequence** with laminated dot-to-dot pictures! Simply place a variety of laminated dot-to-dot activity sheets at your math center, along with dry-erase markers and a box of tissues. Have a student use a marker to follow the dots on a page, using a tissue to erase any mistakes and to clean the page after he's admired the finished picture. Ready for another sheet? There are lots of dots at this center!

Wanda Rikli
Beaver City Elementary
Beaver City, NE

By the Number

Put students in the swim with **number order!** Use the patterns on page 67 to make four fish in each of five different colors for a total of 20 fish. Program each color (school) of fish with numbers for sequencing; then make an answer key. Laminate the fish and the key and then cut them out. Store each color of fish in a separate resealable plastic bag. Place the bags and the answer key at a center. A student sequences the fish in each school and then uses the answer key to check his work.

adapted from an idea by
Dawn Schroeder
Kluckhohn Elementary
LeMars, IA

Woof! Woof!

The unique manipulatives at this math center will have students begging to **sequence numbers** and **count.** To prepare, decorate ten paper bowls to resemble dog food bowls. Label each bowl with a different number from 1 to 10; then place a stuffed animal and a supply of small dog biscuits near the bowls. Direct each child to line up the bowls in numerical order and then place the correct number of bones in each bowl. Bowwow, WOW!

Karen M. Smith
Pace, FL

Number Spin-Off

Here's a partner game that takes students **counting skills** for a spin! Cut apart a copy of the hundred chart on page 81 and mount it on poster board as shown. Also visually divide a tagboard circle into five sections and number them 1 to 5. Laminate the resulting gameboard and spinner wheel. Snap a loose spinner in the center of the spinner wheel; then place the assembled spinner, the gameboard, and two game markers at a center. To play, the partners place their game markers on "1." Then, in turn, each child spins the spinner, moves (in numerical order) the corresponding number of spaces, and reads aloud the number he lands on. The first partner to reach 100 wins!

Kim Wachtel
Sacandaga Elementary
Scotia, NY

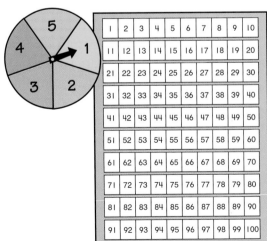

Number & Operations

Ladybug, Ladybug

Science and math crawl right along together in this idea that mingles **number recognition** and ladybugs. For each number that you'd like to include, photocopy a left and right side of a ladybug (page 82) on red construction paper. Program each left side with a dot set, and each right side with a numeral. Also cut out a large construction-paper leaf; then laminate all of the pieces. Store all of the pieces in a decorated string-tie envelope. To do this activity, have a child look through the ladybug pieces. When she finds matching pieces, encourage her to place the matching pairs together on the leaf cutout. Have her continue in the same manner until all the ladybugs are completed.

Regina M. Smith
Glenwood Elementary School
Princeton, WV

Go Fish!

Casting about for a new **number recognition** center? Here's the bait you need. Copy a supply of the fishbowl patterns on page 83 onto blue construction paper. Laminate the fishbowls; then cut them out and program each one with a different numeral. To make goldfish, paint a supply of wooden ice-cream spoons orange. When the paint dries, attach a wiggle eye sticker on each goldfish. Place the fishbowls and the goldfish in a center. To use this center, a child chooses a fishbowl, reads the numeral, and places the corresponding number of goldfish on the bowl.

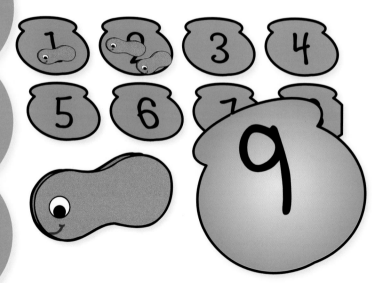

Rachel Meseke Castro
Juneau Elementary
Juneau, WI

Marsha Feffer
Salem Early Childhood Center
Salem, MA

Apple Pickin'

Little ones will be delighted to do this "apple-tizing" **number recognition** center. For each number you would like to include, photocopy the apple, stem, and leaf patterns (page 84) on construction paper. Program each apple with a numeral, each leaf with a number word, and each stem with dots. Laminate the patterns if desired. To use this center, a child matches the corresponding apples, stems, and leaves. Vary this center by providing a large supply of blank construction paper apples so that each child can write the correct numeral on each apple.

Lynette McCaulley Pyne
Plainsboro, NJ

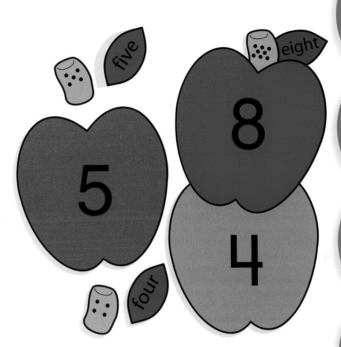

Spotted Giraffes

Here's a fun, hands-on way for youngsters to practice **number recognition** and **counting** skills—while you do a quick spot check of your own! For each numeral you'd like to include, duplicate a copy of the giraffe pattern (page 85) on construction paper. Label each pattern with a different numeral; then cut out and laminate the patterns. To do this activity, ask a child to create play-dough spots equal to the numeral on each giraffe. Have him place the appropriate number of spots on each giraffe. When his work is correct, have the child roll all of the little spots into one ball, ready for the next child to visit the center.

Mary F. Philip
Relay Children's Center
Baltimore, MD

Number & Operations

Spots on Spot

Here's a doggone fun math center to practice **number recognition** and **counting**. For each number that you would like to include in this center, photocopy the dog pattern (page 86). Program each dog's tag with a numeral. Then laminate them. Stock the center with a supply of small black or brown construction paper circles (spots). To use this center, a child chooses a dog, reads the numeral, and then places the corresponding number of spots on the dog cutout.

Laurie Mills
Stevenson Elementary
Stevenson, AL

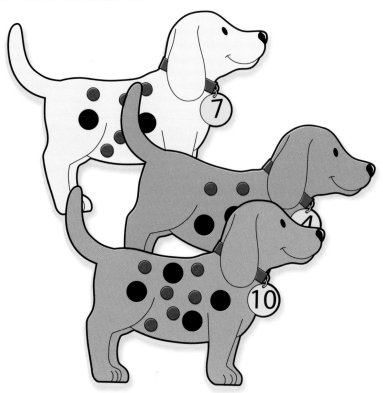

Caterpillar Count

Watch **skip-counting** skills grow right along with these cute caterpillars! To make a caterpillar for skip-counting, cut away the lid of a sterilized egg carton, then cut apart the individual egg cups. Turn each cup over. Decorate one to resemble a caterpillar head and program the remaining cups for skip counting. (Set aside or add extra egg cups as needed.) For self-checking, number the inside of the programmed cups in order (1, 2, 3, ...). Store the cups for each caterpillar in a labeled container or color-code each caterpillar. Working from left to right, a student arranges each set of cups in sequential order, starting with the caterpillar's head. To check his work, he inverts the caterpillar.

Nancy Y. Karpyk
Broadview Elementary
Weirton, WV

Manicure Math

This addition activity will be a favorite—hands down! To prepare, trace a child's hands on a sheet of white paper. Below the hand shapes, write an **addition** sentence as shown, leaving blanks for the numbers. Laminate the paper and place it in your math center, along with a supply of dry-erase markers. Use a white sticky dot to mask the six-dotted side of a die. Place the special die in the center too.

To use this center, a child rolls the die and paints nails (with a marker) on the corresponding number of fingers on the left hand. Then she rolls again and paints the indicated number of nails on the right hand. (If she rolls a blank, she counts it as a zero.) Then she fills in the corresponding numbers to complete the addition sentence. Have her wipe the paper clean and give another manicure for more math fun!

Heather Miller
Creative Playschool
Auburn, IN

$$3 + 2 = 5$$

Chocolate Chip Calculations

Here's an **addition** center students will be eager to sink their teeth into! Cut 20 circles from light brown paper. Use a brown marker to draw one baking chip on each of two blank cutouts. Next, draw two baking chips on each of two blank cutouts. Repeat this procedure for the numbers three through nine. You will have two blank cutouts left. Store the cutouts in a cookie tin, and place it at a center. A student takes two cookies from the tin. On her paper she writes the corresponding addition fact and its answer. To check her work, she counts the chips on the cutouts. She repeats the activity as described until all the cookies are removed from the tin.

Amy Ekmark
Eastside Elementary
Lancaster, CA

Beth

$$2 + 0 = 2$$
$$4 + 6 = 10$$
$$3 + 1 = 4$$

Number & Operations

Buggy Addition

The skill is **addition,** but the appeal is in the bugs! In advance, gather a supply of plastic bugs. Then cut out a large construction paper leaf for a workmat. Draw a thick center vein on the leaf to divide it into two sections; then laminate the leaf. Place blank sheets of paper, the workmat, the bugs, and some pencils in a center. To use this center, a child arranges some bugs on one half of the leaf workmat and some on the other half. Next she writes the number sentence she has just created on a sheet of paper. Then she counts the bugs to determine the answer, and writes it on her paper. She continues making and writing number sentences as desired. Go buggy with addition!

Patricia Draper
Millarville E. C. S.
Millarville, Alberta, Canada

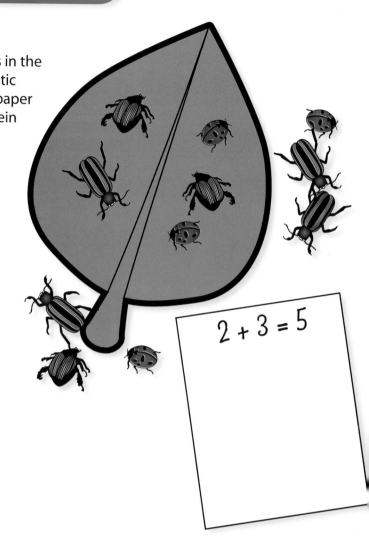

Math Superstars

Do you want your youngsters to be superstars when it comes to **addition** and **subtraction?** All you need are some star stickers and index cards! Affix groups of stickers to a card and draw a plus or minus sign to indicate the operation. Place a variety of cards in a center for youngsters to use. If desired, write the correct answers on the backs of the cards for self-checking.

Rachel Castro
Juneau Elementary
Juneau, WI

Here's the Scoop

Serve up this **addition** activity to help your youngsters master math facts. To prepare, cut cones and scoops of ice cream from construction paper (patterns on page 87). Glue one scoop to the top of each cone. Then program each cone with an addition fact. Place the ice-cream cones and a supply of counters or pom-poms at a center.

Invite each youngster to visit the center and put the correct number of counters or pom-poms on each scoop to represent the fact's answer.

Jennifer Barton
Elizabeth Green School
Newington, CT

"Ssssimple" Sums

Slither into math with this simple **counting** game. Make a copy of the gameboard on page 88 and laminate it for reprogramming. Place the gameboard, two dice, and dry-erase markers at the center. To play the game, each child rolls the dice and counts the number of dots that appear. Then he finds the matching number on the snake and colors that section. When all sections are colored, simply wipe the snake clean for another round of play. "Ssssuper!"

Kyle Welby
Epstein Hebrew Academy
St. Louis, MO

"Sssimple" Sums

10 2 11 3 9 8 4 6 7 5 12

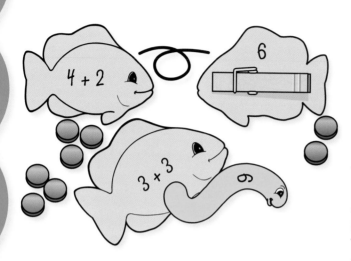

Hooked on Math

Fishing for fun **addition** practice? Hook up to this idea! Begin by duplicating an equal number of the fish and worm patterns (page 89) on construction paper. Program each fish with a simple math problem and each worm with a corresponding answer. Cut out the fish and worms. If desired, program the back of each fish for self-checking; then laminate them. Next hot-glue a clothespin to the back of each fish. Store all these pieces in a plastic fishbowl; then place the fishbowl in a center along with a supply of counters. To use this center, a student chooses a fish, uses the counters to solve the problem, and then clips on the corresponding worm. It's the catch of the day!

Karen Smith
Pace, FL

Frosty Facts

These frosty figures help reinforce **addition** concepts. Photocopy a supply of the snowmen, hats, and snowflakes (page 90) on construction paper. Color and cut out each pattern. Program each snowman with an addition equation that is suitable for your students. Program each hat with a different numeral to correspond to the sum of each addition fact. To use this center, a child chooses a snowman and uses the snowflake manipulatives to work out the problem. When she knows the answer, she places the correspondingly labeled hat on that snowman.

Cindy Stefanick
Roosevelt School
Worcester, MA

Flower Petal Sums

Watch your students' **addition** skills blossom as they practice the commutative property of addition! Tear out the math mat on page 91. Also cut out nine petal shapes from each of two colors of construction paper. Laminate the math mat and the petal cutouts for durability and then store the petals in a resealable plastic bag. Place the mat, the bag of cutouts, addition flash cards, a supply of paper, and pencils at a center. A student selects a math fact and positions petals around the flower center to represent the addends. She records the math fact and its answer on her paper. Next she switches the petals from one flower center to the other to show the inverse of the fact. She records this number sentence on her paper too. She then flips the flash card to check her work. The student continues in this manner until she has solved a predetermined number of math facts.

Kristin McLaughlin
Amity Elementary Center
Douglassville, PA

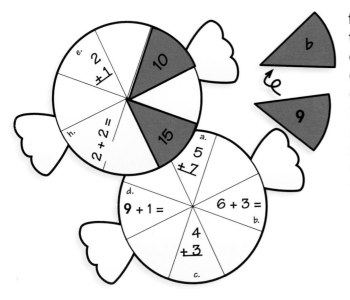

Peppermint Sums

Take a sweet approach to basic **addition** facts! Copy the candy pattern on page 93 to make six white construction paper candies and three red construction paper candies. Program every other section of each white candy with a different alphabet letter and math fact problem. Label the sections of the red candies with the corresponding answers. Cut out each white candy and each red candy section. Code the backs of the red cutouts for self-checking and then laminate the center pieces for durability. Store the cutouts in a holiday tin at a center. A student assembles the peppermint candies. To check her work, she flips the red candy sections. Yummy!

Kacie L. Farmer
Dale, IN

Number & Operations

Grade A Fact Families

Hatch "eggs-tra" practice with **fact families!** Program each of three one-inch tagboard squares with a different number from a chosen fact family. Code the backs of the squares to identify them as a set. Place the squares in a plastic egg and then place the egg in an empty sterilized egg carton. Repeat this process to prepare 11 more eggs for different fact families. Place the egg carton, paper, and pencils at a center. A student removes the squares from a selected egg and writes the corresponding facts. She returns the squares to the empty egg. Then she continues with additional eggs for more Grade-A skill reinforcement!

Antoinette McCoy
Woodside Elementary School
Peekskill, NY

$7 + 5 = 12$
$5 + 7 = 12$
$12 - 5 = 7$
$12 - 7 = 5$

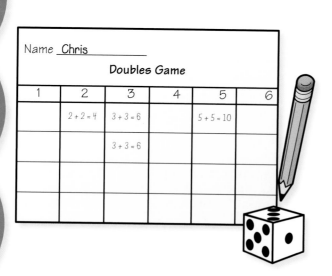

Rolling for Doubles

Count on **doubles facts** to become automatic with this partner game. Prepare student copies of a gameboard similar to the one shown. Place the copies, one die, and pencils at a center. Each player uses a separate gameboard. To take a turn, a player rolls the die. He announces the doubles fact for the number rolled and then writes it in the appropriate column on his gameboard. Alternate play continues until one player has written four doubles facts in one column and is declared the winner. Roll on!

D. Dailey
Garfield School
Ottawa, KS

Half 'n' Half

If your young mathematicians are ready for some **fraction** fun, create this math center activity with the help of your die-cutting machine. Die-cut several pairs of symmetrical shapes from construction paper. Cut one of each pair exactly in half. Make a cut in the other shape from each pair, but make sure it creates two unequal pieces. Glue each cut shape to a large index card, leaving a small gap between the pieces. Then use two of the cards to make the headers as shown. Laminate all the cards and then place them in your math center.

When a child visits this center, he sets out the headers, then sorts the shapes cut in half from those not cut in half. Remind youngsters to look for shapes that have two *equal* parts to help them sort the "halves" from the "halve-nots"!

Kaye Sowell
Pelahatchie Elementary
Brandon, MS

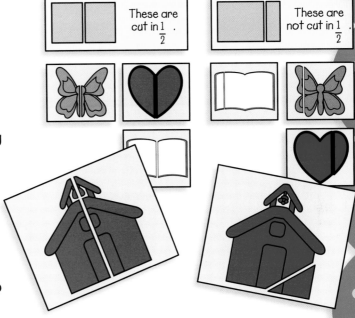

Fraction Creatures

These fun creatures familiarize students with **fractions**—and at the same time, challenge students to think creatively. Place a large supply of one-inch construction paper squares in assorted colors, black fine-tipped markers, a supply of 12" x 18" sheets of drawing paper, and glue at a center. A student folds a sheet of paper in half and in half again; then he unfolds his paper. At the top of each resulting quadrant, he writes a fraction with a denominator of four or less and a color word that describes some of the paper squares at the center. Each quadrant must be labeled differently. Then, in each quadrant, he uses the available supplies to create a creature that represents the quadrant's programming. For example a creature created in a quadrant labeled "2/3 blue" would be made with three paper squares—two of them blue. Fractions have never been more fun!

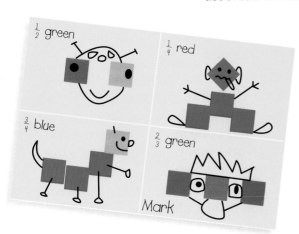

Belinda Darnall Vose
Evergreen Elementary
Ocala, FL

Number & Operations

Place-Value Practice

This daily math center is the place to reinforce beginning **place-value** skills! For each child staple a supply of blank 9" x 12" paper between two 9" x 12" construction paper covers. Have each child personalize his journal and store it in his desk or another desired location. At the center, place several rubber stamps and colorful stamp pads. Each day post a different two-digit number at the center. A student takes his journal to the center and copies the posted number at the top of a blank page. Then he uses a rubber stamp and a stamp pad to program the page with a corresponding set of tens and ones as shown. You can count on this center making a lasting impression on your students!

Michele Lasky Anszelowicz
Mandalay Elementary
Wantagh, NY

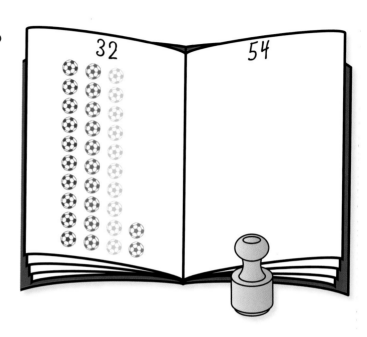

Boning Up

Dish up plenty of practice with **odd and even** numbers! Label construction paper dog-bone patterns (page 94) with odd and even numbers; then laminate the patterns and cut them out. To program the cutouts for self-checking, use a permanent marker to draw an X on the back of each even-numbered bone and an O on the back of each odd-numbered bone. Store the cutouts in a clean and empty dog-bone box. Place the box at a center along with two dog dishes labeled "Odd" and "Even." A student sorts the bones into the dishes and then flips the cutouts to check her work.

Amy Ekmark
Eastside Elementary
Lancaster, CA

1	2	3	4	5	6	7	8	9	10
11	12	13	14	15	16	17	18	19	20
21	22	23	24	25	26	27	28	29	30
31	32	33	34	35	36	37	38	39	40
41	42	43	44	45	46	47	48	49	50
51	52	53	54	55	56	57	58	59	60
61	62	63	64	65	66	67	68	69	70
71	72	73	74	75	76	77	78	79	80
81	82	83	84	85	86	87	88	89	90
91	92	93	94	95	96	97	98	99	100

TEC61024

Ladybug Patterns
Use with "Ladybug, Ladybug" on page 70.

TEC61023

TEC61023

TEC61023

TEC61023

TEC61023

TEC61023

TEC61023

TEC61023

Apple Patterns
Use with "Apple Pickin'" on page 71.

leaf

stem

apple

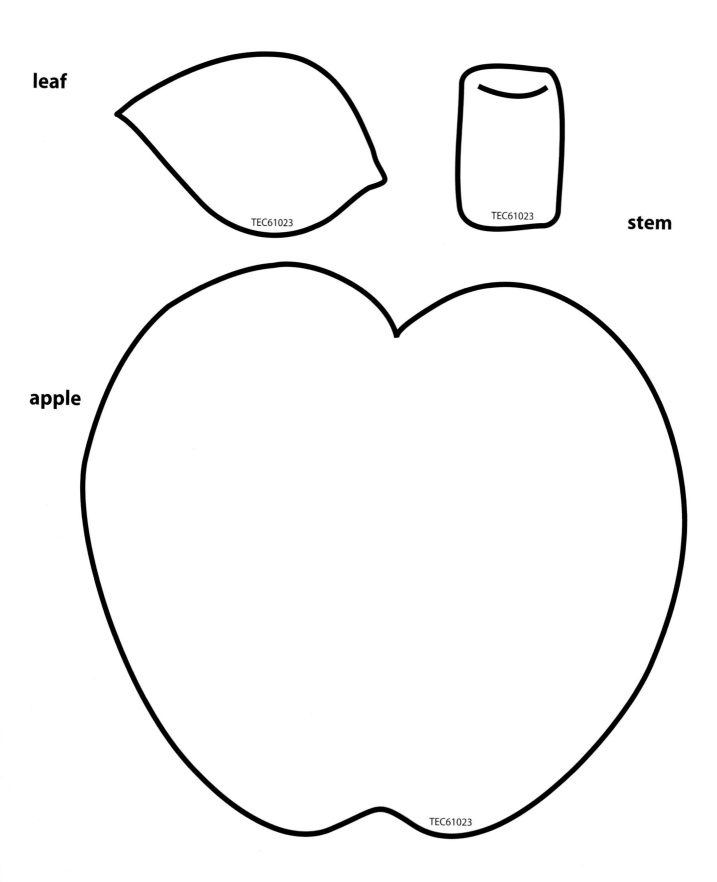

TEC61023

TEC61023

TEC61023

TEC61023

Dog Pattern
Use with "Spots on Spot" on page 72.

TEC61023

TEC61023

TEC61023

TEC61023

"Ssssimple" Sums

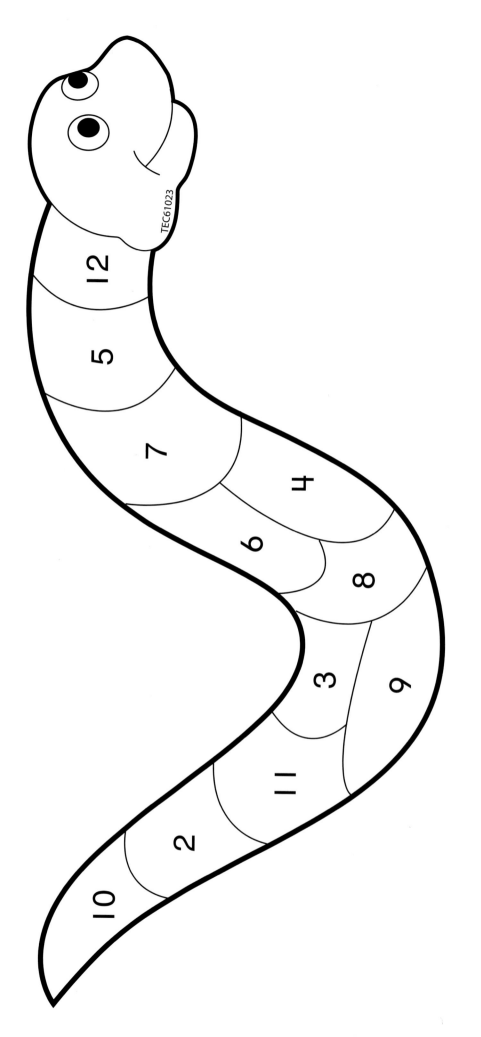

88

Note to the teacher: Use with "Ssssimple Sums" on page 75.

TEC61023

TEC61023

TEC61023

TEC61023

Snowman Patterns

Use with "Frosty Facts" on page 76.

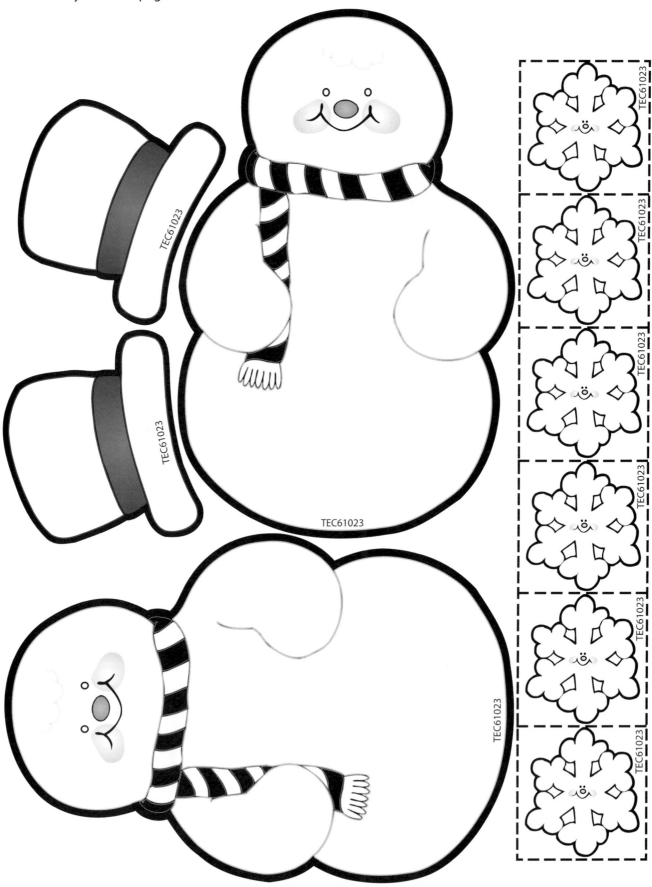

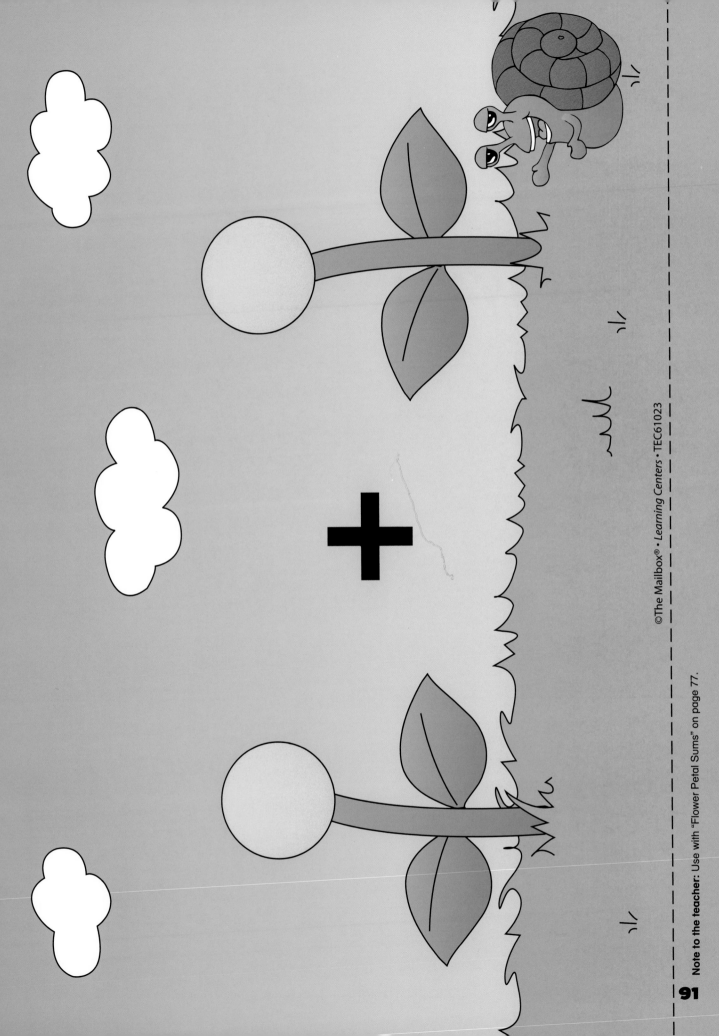

Note to the teacher: Use with "Flower Petal Sums" on page 77.

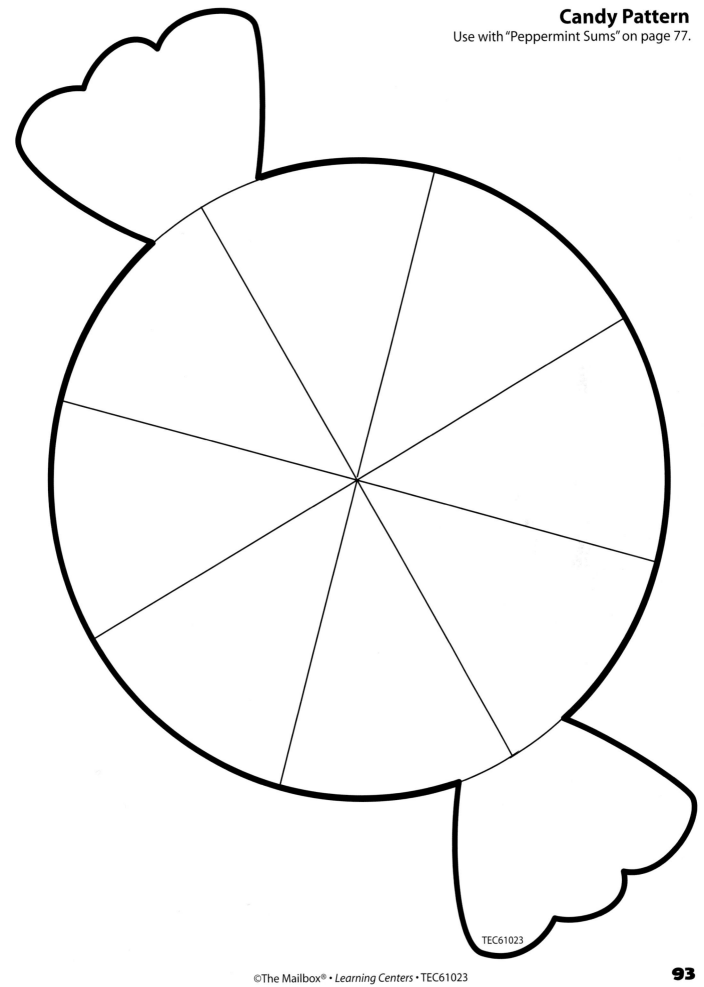

TEC61023

Bone Patterns

Use with "Boning Up" on page 80.

TEC61023

TEC61023

TEC61023

TEC61023

Measurement Station

Give students ongoing practice with seriation by setting up a measurement station in your math area. Label two sides of a desk or tabletop with the words *shortest* and *longest*. Then program a sentence strip, as shown, inserting the word for whatever items you provide at the center. Place a cupful of pencils, crayons, sticks, carrots, or other items on the desk. Then ask a child to compare the items and line them up on the tabletop from shortest to longest. Keep a list of student names nearby so that each child can check off her name as she visits the station. Change the measurement item weekly to keep student interest high.

Karen Walker
LaCroft Elementary
Liverpool, OH

"Bat-rrr" Up!

Here's a **nonstandard measurement** activity your youngsters will go batty over. For each child, make a construction paper copy of the bat measuring tape on page 98. Also make a class supply of the recording sheet on page 99. Place these items in a center along with some scissors and glue. Help each child cut and glue the pieces of the measuring tape where indicated. Challenge the child to use her bat tape to measure each object in your classroom that is pictured on the recording sheet. Have her write the results on her paper.

Sherry Fenton
Petroglyph Elementary
Albuquerque, NM

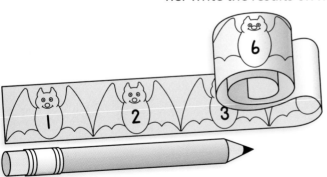

Measurement

How Many Scoops?

Little ones will get lots of practice estimating **capacity** in this center. Provide a large tub half-filled with colored, uncooked rice. Place funnels, different-size plastic containers, and scoops near the tub. To use this center, a student pair chooses a scoop and a container. One child places a funnel in the container; then he and his partner each estimate how many scoops of rice it will take to fill the container. Next the pair scoops rice into the funnel in the container while both students count each scoop. Each student compares his estimate to the actual number of scoops it took to fill the container.

Debbie Earley
Mountain View Elementary
Kingsley, PA

Pasta Procedure

Help your youngsters practice **capacity, estimation,** and **counting** with this neat noodle center! To prepare, make a class supply of the recording sheet on page 100. Place the sheets at your math center, along with a corresponding set of measuring cups and a full cup of uncooked pasta, such as bow-tie or rotini. Have a child at this center first measure the pasta into the one-cup measuring cup. Have him record his estimation of how many pieces are in the cup. Then have him count the pasta to determine the actual answer. Have him repeat the procedure with the ½-cup, ⅓-cup, and ¼-cup measuring cups.

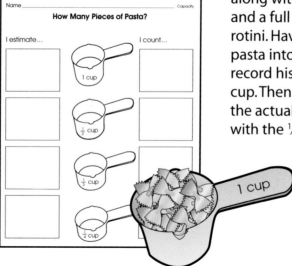

Carole Beckman
Sea Gate Elementary
Naples, FL

Pocket Change

This versatile center activity is a great investment in your youngsters' **money-counting** skills. Copy several construction paper pocket patterns from page 101 and cut them out. Glue them onto a sheet of tagboard titled "Pocket Change." Number the pockets and then laminate the poster for durability. Use Sticky-Tac or tape to attach a desired combination of paper coins to each pocket. Program an answer key and then place the poster, answer key, and a supply of blank paper at a center. A student numbers her paper and writes how much change is in the corresponding pocket.

To reprogram the activity, modify the coin combination on each pocket and provide a corresponding answer key. Now that's a "cent-sational" center!

Sherrie Rippy
Van Duyn Elementary
Clinton, IN

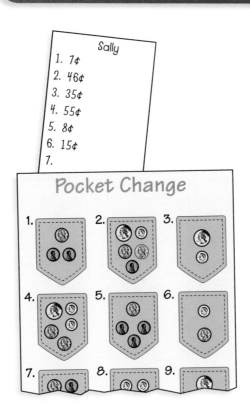

Right on the Money

Three little piggies can provide a wealth of **money-counting** practice! Use the pattern on page 102 to make three pink construction paper pigs. Write a different price on each pig; then cut out the patterns. Place the cutouts, stamp pads, a set of coin stamps, pencils, and blank paper at a center. A student writes the price of one pig on his paper and then he stamps three (or more) different coin combinations that equal the price on the pig. He repeats the process for each remaining pig. Oink!

Jill Hamilton
Schoeneck Elementary
Stevens, PA

Bat Measuring Tape

Use with "'Bat-rrr' Up!" on page 95.

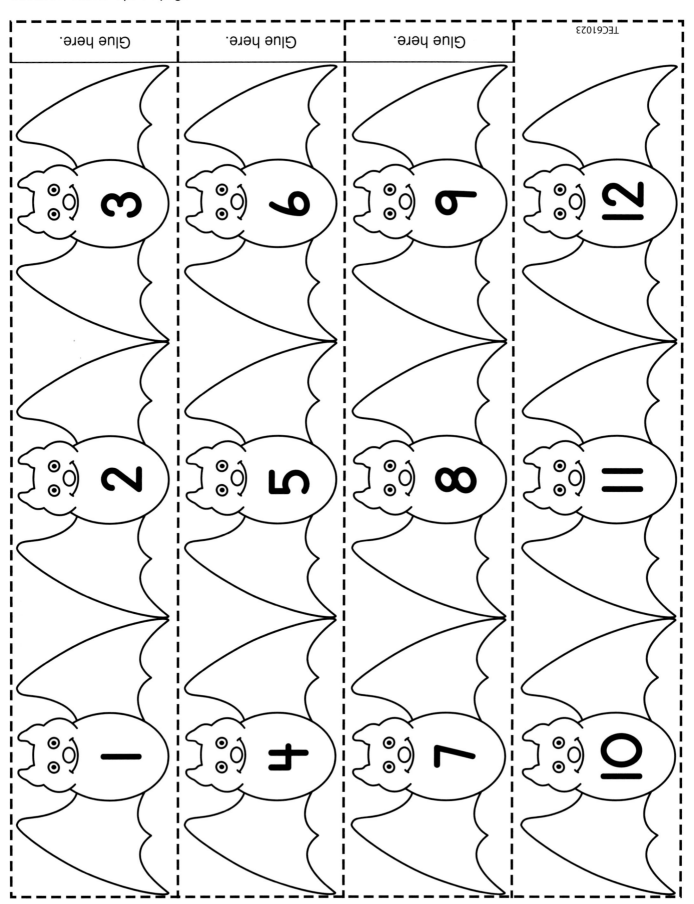

Name _____

_____ bats

_____ bats

_____ bats

_____ bats

_____ bats

_____ bats

Note to the teacher: Use with "'Bat-rrr' Up!" on page 95.

How Many Pieces of Pasta?

I estimate...   I count...

1 cup

$\frac{1}{2}$ cup

$\frac{1}{3}$ cup

$\frac{1}{4}$ cup

Note to the teacher: Use with "Pasta Procedure" on page 96.

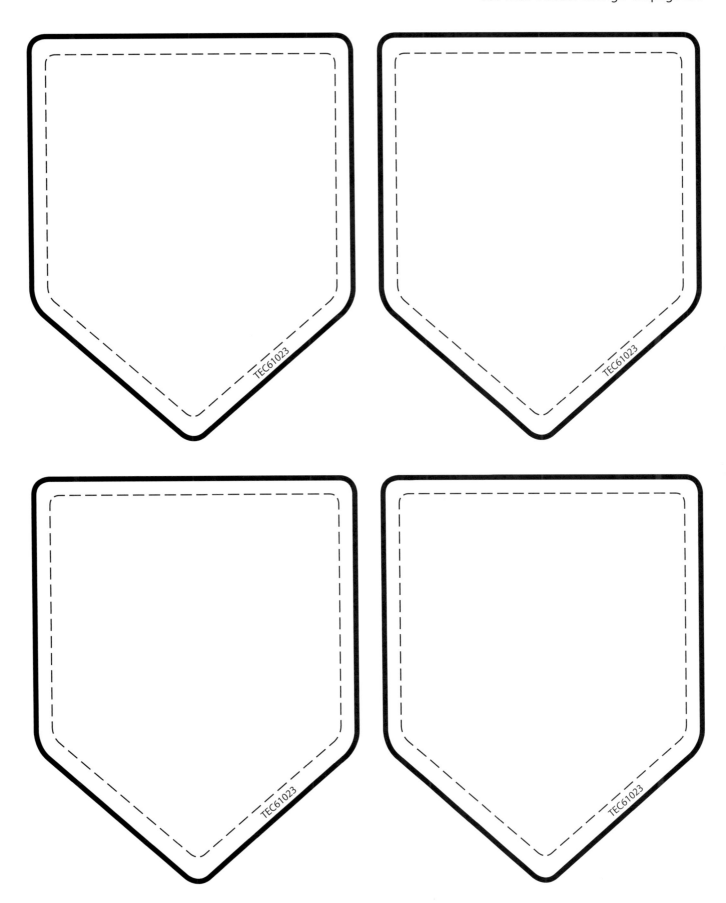

TEC61023

TEC61023

TEC61023

TEC61023

Pig Pattern

Use with "Right on the Money" on page 97.

TEC61023

Shaping Up

Use this center idea to help young-sters recognize **shapes** in everyday objects. To prepare, cut out the picture cards on pages 104 and 105. Laminate them for durability. Next, program a piece of poster board similar to the one shown. Place the cards near the poster board and invite students to sort the cards onto the poster board by shape. This slice of pizza looks like a triangle!

Quazonia Quarles
Girls Inc.
Newark, DE

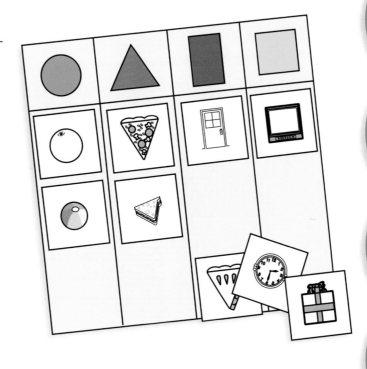

Shapely Snowpals

Even if snow isn't in the forecast, your students will have plenty of frosty fun creating snowpals from **shapes!** Place glue and a supply of each of the following construction paper cutouts at a center: 8-inch white circles (faces), $4\frac{1}{2}$" x $5\frac{1}{2}$" black rectangles (hats), $1\frac{1}{2}$" x 9" black rectangles (hat brims), 3" x 9" colorful rectangles (scarves), and an assortment of small circles (eyes) and triangles (noses, mouths, and scarf fringe). Ask each student to use these materials to create a snowpal like the one shown. Then have each child write the number of circles, triangles, and rectangles he used on the back of his project. What a fun way to shape up geometry skills!

Becky Shelley
Anderson Elementary
Anderson, MO

Picture Cards

Use with "Shaping Up" on page 103.

TEC61023

TEC61023

TEC61023

CRAYONS

TEC61023

TEC61023

TEC61023

TEC61023

JUICE

TEC61023

TEC61023

TEC61023

A

A

TEC61023

TEC61023

TEC61023

TEC61023

TEC61023

TEC61023

TEC61023

TEC61023

ADMIT ONE

TEC61023

TEC61023

Graphing

Sticker Race

Your little race fans will love this **graphing** activity! To prepare, collect a supply of six different designs of small incentive-chart stickers (often sold in packages of six designs). Attach a different sticker to each side of a blank die or small cube. Then cut apart the remaining stickers in strips of six different designs. Next photocopy a class set of the graph on page 107. Place the graphs, sticker strips, and die in a math center. When a child visits this center, have him take one sticker strip and place a different sticker at the bottom of each graph column. To start the race, have the child roll the die and check to see which sticker faces up. Instruct him to color a square in the corresponding column. Have him continue in the same manner until one column is completely colored. When any column reaches the top, that sticker is the winner!

Barbara Steelman
Rosary Catholic School
Oklahoma City, OK

Spin and Graph

Little ones will be spinning their way to **graphing** skills with this fun independent activity. To prepare, make a supply of the graphing sheet on page 108. Create a spinner by cutting a five-inch circle from tagboard. Divide the circle into five sections and glue a different shell (cut from one copy of the graphing sheet) onto each section. Add a metal spinner mechanism to the circle's center. (Or simply attach the shell cutouts to an existing spinner with five sections.) Place the graphing sheets, the spinner, crayons, and a timer in your math center.

To use this center, a child sets the timer for a specified amount of time, such as five minutes. She spins and then colors in a matching shell on her graphing sheet. She continues to spin and color until the timer goes off. Then she examines her graph to see which shell she had the most and the fewest of and if she had an equal number of any shells. Have her share her findings with you so you can assess her grasp of graphing.

Linda Havens
Parkwood-Upjohn Elementary
Kalamazoo, MI

Name _____

Sticker Race

Note to the teacher: Use with "Sticker Race" on page 106.

Name

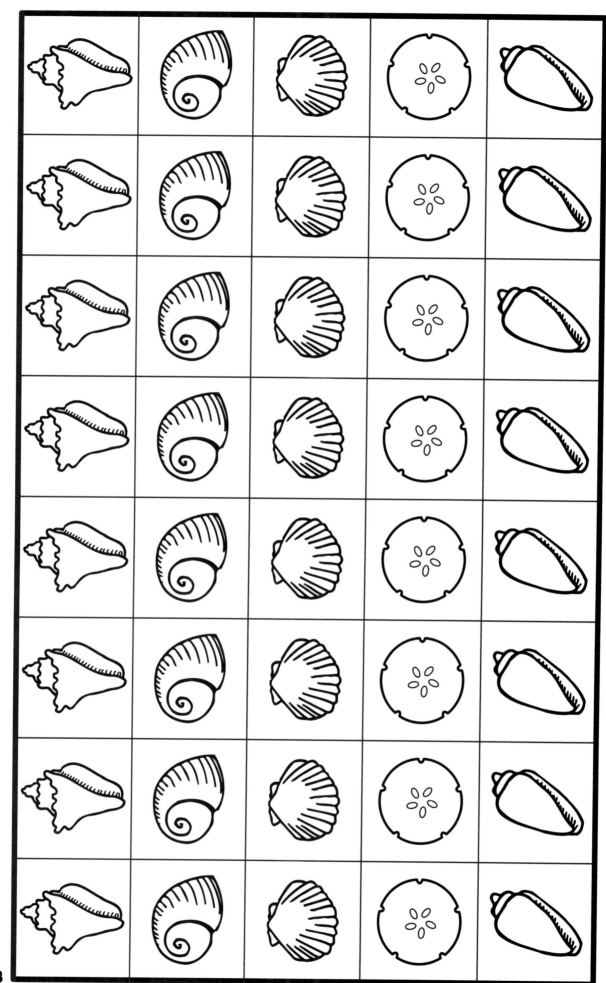

Note to the teacher: Use this page with "Spin and Graph" on page 106.

Pattern Cans

Take those chip cans from potatoes to **patterning**! To make a pattern can, cover a clean potato chip can with white paper. Then lay the can on its side and draw a simple pattern along the length of the can. Drop the matching manipulatives inside the can and pop the top back on. You might use counting cubes, teddy bear counters, cereal pieces, or links. At your math center, have each child pour out the manipulatives and then copy and extend the pattern on a tabletop.

Toni Osterbuhr
Price-Harris Elementary
Wichita, KS

Lots of Scoops

To prepare this **patterning** center, draw a large ice-cream cone on a 12" x 18" sheet of construction paper. Then cut some scoops of ice cream (sized to fit the cone) from various colors of construction paper. Make patterning cards by drawing ice-cream cones with various scoop color patterns on index cards. Laminate the cone, the scoops, and the patterning cards for durability. Then slip the scoops and cards into a two-pocket folder for easy storage. A child at this center chooses a patterning card and then creates the matching pattern with the large scoops and cone. Before you know it, little ones will have patterning practice licked!

Lisa Mascheri
Midway Elementary
Sanford, FL

Patterning

A-Patterning We Will Go

This center provides a great activity that reinforces **patterning** skills. Stock the center with a supply of multiples of classroom items such as pencils, erasers, rulers, and large paper clips. To use this center, a child arranges some of the items to make a pattern of his choice. Vary this activity by having one child begin a pattern and having a second child finish it.

Rochie Kogan
Yeshiva Ohr Yisroel
Forest Hills, NY

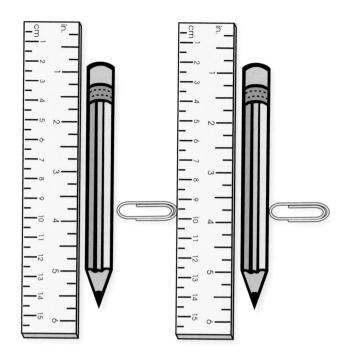

Ice-Cube Tray Patterns

Little ones will be delighted to visit this cool **patterning** center. Stock your center with a bowl of different-colored pom-poms and several ice-cube trays. Encourage children to visit this center in pairs. Instruct each child in a pair to arrange pom-poms in one side of a different tray, making the color pattern of his choice. Then have the children in the pair switch trays and duplicate the pattern in their partner's tray.

Terri Whitaker
Barrington Place
Sugar Land, TX

S-S-Slide Into Patterns

Slide in some **patterning** practice as your youngsters create this slithery snake! Stock a center with various colors of construction paper cut into 2" x 5" strips and a class supply of yarn pieces that are three feet long. Demonstrate how to glue the ends of a paper strip together to form a link. Then review with your students an AB pattern (such as red, blue, red, blue) and an ABC pattern (such as red, blue, green, red, blue, green).

To make a snake, each child arranges ten colored links in his chosen pattern on the table and then tapes one end of the yarn inside the last link. Next, he slides the yarn through the remaining links and tapes it inside the first link. Finally, the child adds wiggle eye stickers and a felt tongue as shown. Invite each student to hold up his wiggly snake and describe its pattern to the class.

Lorrie Hartnett
Tom Green Elementary
Buda, TX

Barnyard Math

What's down at the farm? Kid-pleasing **number patterns**! Cover the bottom and lid of an empty shoebox with red paper. Draw details so that the box resembles a barn. Place at least four small plastic hens and cows (or other two- and four-legged farm animals) inside. Then put the lid on the box. Design a recording sheet similar to the one shown. Copy it to make a class supply. Place the copies, box, and pencils at a center. A student examines the farm animals and fills in the blanks on her sheet. For each column of totals, she writes a sentence to describe the pattern.

How Many Legs? — Annie

1 hen	**2** legs	1 cow ___ legs
2 hens	**4** legs	2 cows ___ legs
3 hens	**6** legs	3 cows ___ legs
4 hens	___ legs	4 cows ___ legs

Rebecca Brudwick
Hoover Elementary
North Mankato, MN

111

Where Do Vegetables Grow?

Your little gardeners will use a variety of skills with this vegetable investigation. Gather a supply of plastic or real vegetables, such as carrots, potatoes, beets, celery, lettuce, onions, cauliflower, and broccoli. Then place them at a center.

Invite each child to observe the vegetables and sort them into two groups, those that grow *above* ground and those that grow *below* ground. Or for more of a challenge, have each youngster sort the vegetables into groups of *roots, stems,* and *flowers.* Is that some critical thinking beginning to sprout?

Connie Templeton
Huntington Beach, CA

A Growing Greenhouse

These greenhouses will cause youngsters to grow roots in your science center. Cut out a tagboard copy of the house template on page 121. Have each child fold a 12" x 18" sheet of green construction paper in half. Help the child trace the house template onto his paper, positioning the roof along the fold. Instruct the child to cut along the house outline through both thicknesses of paper and then cut out the window only through the top sheet. If desired, encourage the child to decorate his house and label it with his name. Provide each child with a quart-size resealable plastic bag, a damp paper towel, and three lima beans. Have him fold the paper towel and put it in his bag. Then have him place the lima beans between the towel and the bag. Seal the bag and staple it to the bottom house shape so that the seeds show through the window. Encourage each child to draw pictures and record the daily changes happening in his greenhouse in a science journal. There's a lot of learning sprouting up!

Brenda S. Beard
Greenbrier Elementary
Greenbrier, TN

Sorting Animals

Boost beginning classification skills with this idea! Cut apart the animal pictures on page 115. Make a chart with the headings "Farm Animals" and "Not Farm Animals." Place the chart and animal pictures in your science center, along with some nonfiction books about farm animals. Have students examine the animals and sort them onto the chart, using the books for reference if needed.

Kim Lockley
Hawk Ridge Elementary
Charlotte, NC

Floral Clay? OK!

The next time you want your little ones to experiment with items that sink or float, bring in some floral clay. Demonstrate that a ball of the clay sinks. Then invite youngsters to shape the clay to try to make it float. (This clay will float if shaped like a boat, and it won't dissolve or make a mess.) When the experiment is over, dry the clay and store it in a plastic bag. It lasts and lasts!

Ronda Caster
Supply Elementary
Supply, NC

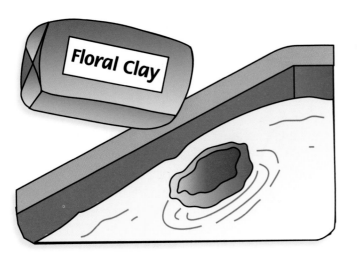

Four Seasons' Fashions

Your little ones will use their classification and critical-thinking skills as they dress for seasonal success with this file folder activity. Make four brown construction paper copies of the bear pattern below. Cut out the four bears and then glue them to the inside of a file folder. Label the area below each bear with a different season as shown. Cut out the clothing and accessories on pages 117 and 119. Next, laminate the folder and the cutouts for durability; then store everything in a large zippered plastic bag. To complete the activity, a child opens the folder and dresses each bear with appropriate clothing (and accessories) for the season.

Felicia Dannick-Friedman
Children's Discovery Center
Columbia, MD

Bear Pattern
Use with "Four Seasons' Fashions" above.

TEC61023

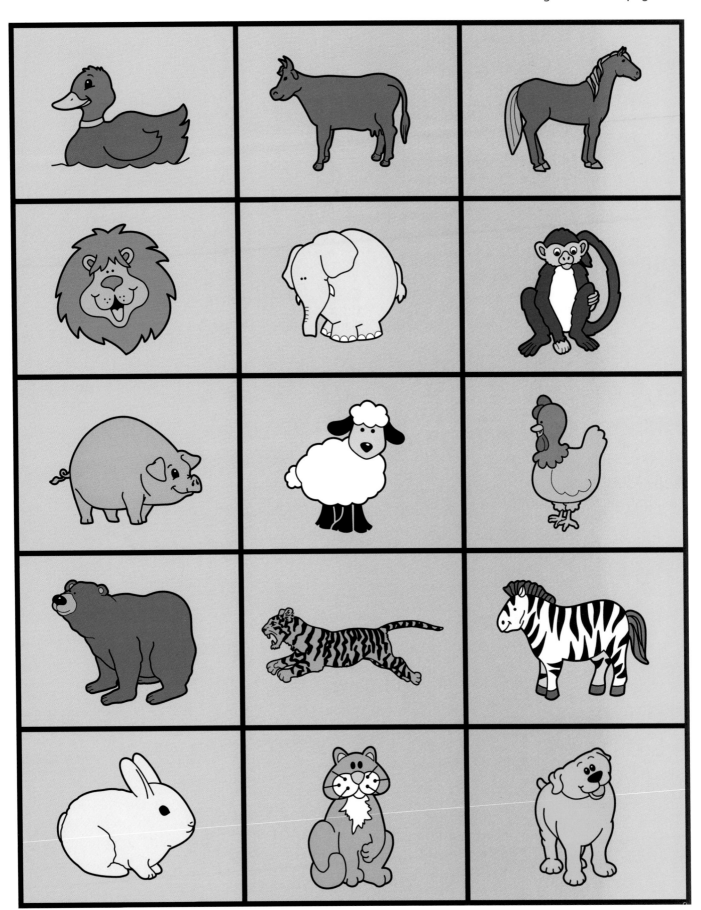

farm animal	farm animal	farm animal
TEC61023	TEC61023	TEC61023
TEC61023	TEC61023	TEC61023
farm animal	farm animal	farm animal
TEC61023	TEC61023	TEC61023
TEC61023	TEC61023	TEC61023
farm animal	farm animal	farm animal
TEC61023	TEC61023	TEC61023

Cut out.

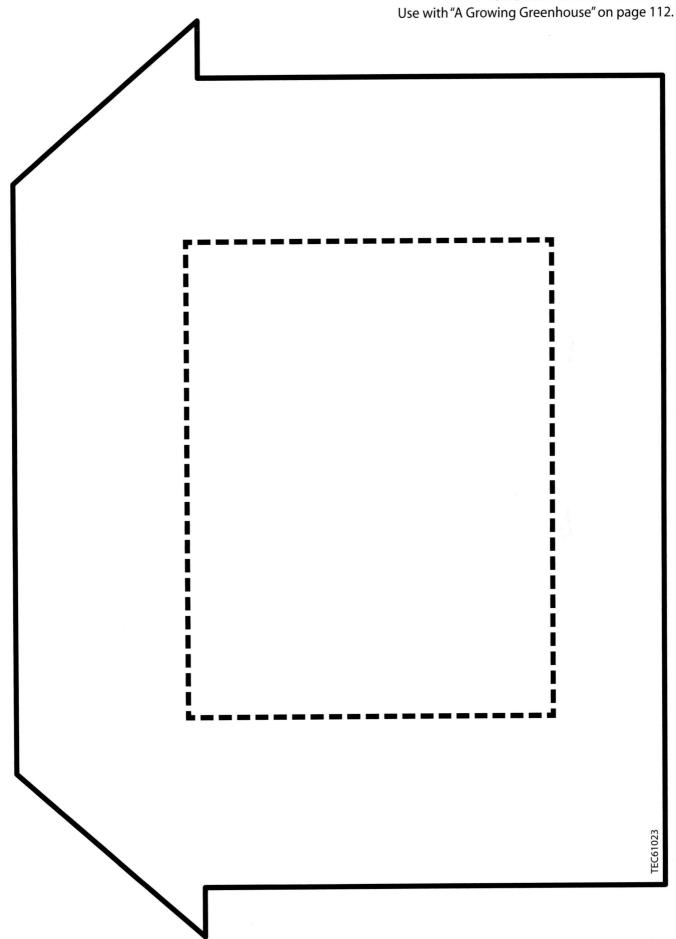

TEC61023

Fine Motor

Children and the Chocolate Factory

Set up a chocolate factory in your fine-motor or art center! In advance, mix up a batch or two of chocolate-scented play dough by adding a few tablespoons of baking cocoa to your favorite play-dough recipe. Then arrange the play dough in a center along with rolling pins, plastic knives, spatulas, and pastel-colored work-mats. When children visit this center, remind them that this play dough is not edible. Then encourage each child to create the ultimate chocolate creation. Mmm—this chocolatey center sure smells fun!

Lori Kent
Hood River, OR

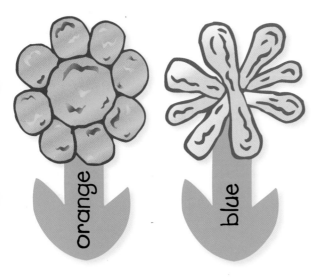

Blooming With Color

Color words are in full bloom here! Program a supply of construction paper stems with different color words. Then set out the corresponding colors of play dough (or colors that can be mixed to make the corresponding colors). Each child who visits this center chooses a stem and then makes a flower that's the matching color. What a bouquet of learning!

adapted from an idea by Kristi Kruft
Mary Walter Elementary
Bealeton, VA

Geoboard Jamboree

Get little fingers moving and young minds working at this center! Make a set of cards showing letters, numbers, and shapes. Put the cards in your fine-motor area, along with Geoboards and rubber bands. Have each child choose a card and then use rubber bands to form the symbol or shape on it. As an added challenge, ask her to count the number of rubber bands she uses to form each letter, number, or shape.

Jaclyn Scott
John Muir Elementary
Glendale, CA

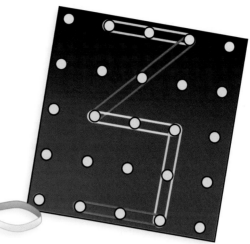

Color Drops

Little fingers will get a fine-motor workout at this color exploration center. In advance, collect some sterilized foam egg cartons. Place them in a center along with at least three eyedroppers and red, blue, and yellow colored water. When a child visits this center, invite her to squeeze one colored-water drop at a time into the egg cups, mixing and matching the colors as she likes. Encourage children to try to make new colors and share their discoveries with each other.

Tara Stefanich
Merritt Elementary
Mt. Iron, MN

Fine Motor

Pound Out a Pattern

Strengthen fine-motor skills as patterns pop up at this fun center. In advance, collect a supply of colored golf tees, foam blocks, and toy hammers. Use markers to create simple color patterns on white index cards. Put the golf tees and pattern cards in the center. Secure the foam blocks to a table with Sticky-Tac. To use the center, each child chooses a card and re-creates the pattern by hammering the matching colored golf tees into the foam. As a variation, ask students to pound golf tees in a high and low pattern as shown.

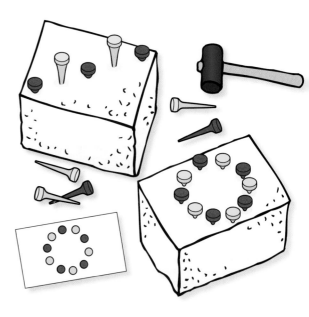

Marcia Boone and Robin Gattis
Seagoville Elementary School
Seagoville, TX

Just a Dot

Do your youngsters need some gluing practice? Try making some dazzling dots to reinforce that just a bit of glue is plenty! First, talk with students about why they only need a small dot of glue for most gluing projects. Have them chant "Not a lot, just a dot!" several times. Then bring out a supply of 1" x 6" construction paper strips. Invite each youngster to make dots of glue on a strip. If any dots turn into puddles, toss the strip and give the child a new one. Reward all those just-right dots of glue with a sprinkle of glitter. Then, when the glue dries, staple the strip around the child's wrist so he may wear it home. If desired, coordinate the paper strip and glitter to match your school colors!

Toni Osterbuhr
Price-Harris School
Wichita, KS

Pretty Portraits

Turn your art center into a portrait studio with this "bear-y" good idea. Place a large teddy bear on a stool beside the painting easel. Put a prop box nearby with clothing, accessories, and other items that can be used to dress the bear. Have each child outfit the bear any way she chooses. Then encourage her to paint a portrait of her fuzzy friend. After all the paintings are dry, display them together to create a gallery of fine art.

Wendy Rapson
Kids in Action, Hingham
Hingham, MA

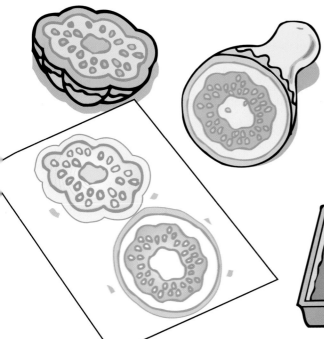

Gourd Prints

This art center is a prime place for making gourd prints. In advance, cut various gourds in half. Pour tempera paints into shallow pans. Place the gourds, sheets of large construction paper, and the paints in a center. To use this center, a child dips a gourd into a color of paint and then presses it onto a sheet of construction paper. Have him continue in this manner, making the designs of his choice.

Katie Gaie
Parkview Elementary
Plymouth, WI

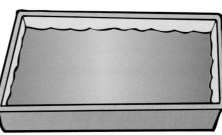

Art

Paint Palettes

Your little artists will have a grand time learning about mixing colors at this center. Stock the center with a classroom supply of palette cutouts, paintbrushes, and red, blue, and yellow paint. To use this center, have a child use a different paintbrush to paint one dab each of red, blue, and yellow paint onto his palette. Encourage each child to use his fingers to mix different colors of paint on different spots on his palette. For example, on one spot he may mix yellow paint with red paint. What color did you get? "Color-rific!"

Daphne M. Orenshein
Yavneh Hebrew Academy
Los Angeles, CA

Hexagons and Honeycombs

This tracing activity will have your students buzzing with excitement! Provide hexagonal pattern blocks, paper, pencils, and crayons at a center. Have each student trace the pattern blocks over and over to create a honeycomb design on his paper. When the page is full, invite him to draw and color bees in the honeycomb cells.

Connie Collins
Walls Elementary School
Walls, MS

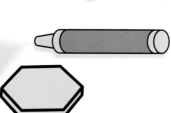

Dramatic Play

Get Fit!

Students will become fitness buffs while visiting this workout center. To set up the center, place floor mats, lightweight wrist and ankle weights, and a CD player with upbeat music in your dramatic-play area. Demonstrate how to use the weights; then encourage each student to visit the center to stretch, flex, and build her muscles. For added interest, play children's exercise videos; then watch your little ones join right in and get fit!

Bonnie Elizabeth Vontz
Cheshire Country Day School
Milldale, CT

Pizza-Parlor Pizzazz

Fill your dramatic-play center with all the props needed to create a pizza restaurant; then watch youngsters ooze with pizza-parlor savvy. Supply the center with empty pizza boxes, cardboard pizza rounds to use as crusts, and felt or construction paper toppings—such as pepperoni, green peppers, and shredded cheese. If desired, store each of the ingredients in a separate resealable plastic bag. Add hot mitts, aprons, dishes, eating utensils, rolling pins, toy pizza cutters, and clean plastic soda bottles to the center. Display laminated pizza pictures (cut from frozen pizza boxes); then invite small groups of students, in turn, to set up and operate their own pizza parlor. Now that's pizza with pizzazz!

Jackie Meyer
Eden Prairie, MN

Dramatic Play

Kids in the Candy Store

Set up this candy store in your dramatic-play area. Put a cash register and some play money, as well as napkins and paper plates in the center. Have students help you make candy from play dough or clay. To make lollipops, roll the clay into long snakes, coil them, and add craft stick handles. Also press clay or dough into candy molds (sold at your local craft store). Be sure to stock the center with some waxed paper so students can wrap their candy creations. And, of course, add some empty candy boxes for those who want to buy a special someone a selection of sweet treats!

Jennifer Feldmann
Walnut Creek Day School
Columbia, MO

Prescription for Learning

Need to reinforce a variety of skills? This center is just what the doctor ordered. Contact parents, your doctor's office, and a local hospital for donations of the items listed below. Set up an examination room, a waiting area, and a reception desk. Place doctor-related books, such as *My Doctor, My Friend* by P. K. Hallinan and *Too Big!* by Claire Masurel, in the waiting area. The doctor will see you now for some reading, writing, and dramatic-play fun!

Possible items to include:

surgical gowns	bandages
clipboard	telephone
surgical masks	paper
growth chart	pens
eye chart	notepads
toy doctor's kit	scale
stethoscope	dolls

Kay Dawson
Newport News, VA